Culinary Masterpieces Made Easy

by Stephen Blancett

Text and photographs copyright © 2021 by Stephen Blancett.
All rights reserved.

No part of this book may be reproduced in any written, electronic, recording or photocopying without written permission of the publisher or author. The exception would be in the case of brief quotations embodied in the critical articles or reviews and pages in which permission is specifically granted by the publisher or author.

Although every precaution has been taken to verify the accuracy of the information contained herein, the author and publisher assume no responsibility for any errors or omissions. No liability is assumed for damages that may result from the use of information contained within.

Books may be purchased by visiting:
ArtistInTheKitchen.com

Cover and Interior Design: Advertising.Design, LLC

Publisher: Gallery.International, LLC

Editor: Randy Kambic

ISBN: 978-0-578-31947-6

First Edition

Printed in the United States of America.

James,

Thank you for the many years of encouragement.

Thank you for always believing in me.

Thank you for being the "guinea pig"
for every recipe in this book.

Thank you for the honest feedback and input.

Thank you for inspiring me to be my best.

Thank you for the endless laughs.

Thank you for being cray-cray with me.

My world is brighter and
more beautiful because of you.

Got Courage

Contents

Foreword 3
Introduction 5
Acknowledgments 7

Appetizers 9
   Pastry-Wrapped Baked Brie 10
     with Sautéed Plums and Shallots
   Fried Green Tomatoes with 12
     Spicy Remoulade Sauce
   Caribbean Conch Fritters 14
     with Orange Aioli
   Shrimp Ceviche 16
   Beer-Battered Fried Pickles 18
     with Spicy Ranch Dressing
   Spicy Black-Eyed Pea Hummus 20

Breakfast and Brunch 23
   Hawaiian Pancakes 24
   Bacon-Kale Egg Breakfast Muffins . . . 26
     with Sun-Dried Tomatoes
   Eggs Benedict with Prosciutto 28
   Smoked Salmon Eggs Benedict 30
     with Pan-Seared Tomatoes
     and Asparagus
   Dutch Baby Pancake with 32
     Blackberries and Sliced Almonds
   Ham and Cheese Casserole 34
     with Hash Brown Crust

Soups, Stews and Chili 37
   Caribbean Beef Pepperpot Stew 38
   Spicy African Chicken Peanut Stew . . . 40

U.S. Senate Bean Soup 42
French Onion Soup 44
Creamy Potato Mushroom Soup 46
Asparagus Bisque 48
Caribbean Coconut-Curry 50
   Sweet Potato Soup
Creamy and Cheesy 52
   Sausage Potato Soup
Avgolemono 54
   (Greek Lemon Chicken Soup)

Salads 57
   German Roasted 58
     Purple Potato Salad
   Sweet and Sour Three-Bean Salad . . . 60
   Tomato Carpaccio 62
     with Honey Dijon Vinaigrette
   Spring Greens Salad with Pecan- 64
     Crusted Tofu and Mojito Dressing
   Wasabi Honey Coleslaw 66
   Roasted Beet Salad with Apples, ... 68
     Feta and Candied Walnuts
   Bloody Mary Shrimp 70
     and Pasta Salad

Vegetables and Sides 73
   Baked Mashed Potatoes 74
   Mofongo 76
     (Puerto Rican-Style Plantains)
   Festive Fondant Potatoes 78
   Mashed Purple Sweet Potatoes with . . 80
     Coconut Milk, Lime and Ginger

German Spätzle/Spaetzle 82
(Tiny Egg Noodle Dumplings)

Portobello Stuffed Cabbage 84

Buttery, Crispy, Parmesan-Herbed 86
Potato Stacks

Incredible Bacon-Wrapped 88
Mac and Cheese

Classic German 90
Red Cabbage (Rotkohl)

Burgers 93

Smoked Sirloin, Brie, Bacon Burgers ... 94
with Merlot-Portabellos

Caribbean Burgers 96
with Tropical Fruit Salsa

Gyro-Inspired Greek Lamb 98
Burgers with Tzatziki Yogurt

Hot Buffalo, Bacon, Blue Burgers 100
with Celery Salsa

Thanksgiving Turkey Burgers 102
with Stuffing and
Cranberry Sauce

Meat 105

Flank Steak with 106
Avocado Chimichurri Sauce

Palomilla Steak 108

Stir-Fried Beef and Vegetables 110

German Sauerbraten 112

Asian-Style Pepper Steak 114

Mshikaki Steak Kebabs with 116
Tomato Onion Sauce

Philly Steak Mac and Cheese 118

Rich and Creamy Beef Stroganoff ... 120

Irish Shepherd's Pie 122
with Beef Tenderloin Tips

Lime Chicken with 124
Blueberry Bourbon Sauce

Papaya Chicken Curry 126
with Coconut Rice

Chicken Piccata 128

Artichoke Chicken 130
with Bow Tie Pasta

Sesame-Ginger Chicken 132

Firecracker Chicken 134

Tequila-Lime Chicken Tacos 136
with Creamy Cilantro-
Jalapeño Sauce

Coconut Pineapple Chicken 138
with Coconut Rice

Savory Ginger Chicken 140
Thighs and Drumsticks

Coconut-Peanut 142
Curry Chicken

Creamy Garlic Chicken Pasta 144
with Zucchini and Yellow Squash

Lemon Chicken 146

Slow Cooker Mojo Pork Roast 148

Caribbean Pork Chops with 150
Spicy Lime-Rum Jerk Sauce

Hot Dog Skillet Casserole 152

Orange Marmalade Pork Chops 154

Orange-Ginger Glazed Pork Chops .. 156

Root Beer-Glazed Baby Back Ribs ... 158

Rosemary-Dijon Pork Chops 160

San Francisco Pork Chops 162

Pork Tenderloin with 164
Seared Pears and Shallots

Caribbean-Spiced Pork 166
Tenderloin with Pineapple-
Mint Salsa

Roasted Pork Loin with 168
Apples, Pears and Prunes

Black-Eyed Peas with Sausage, ... 170
Ham Hocks and Bacon

Lamb Chops with 172
  Garlic-Mint Sauce
Herb-Crusted Lamb Chops 174
  with Raspberry Sauce

Seafood 177
Sesame-Crusted Tuna 178
  with Mango Salsa
Coconut Shrimp with 180
  Orange Sauce
Lump Crab Cakes 182
  with Chipotle Sauce
Southern Shrimp and 184
  Cheesy Grits
Coconut Curry Soup 186
  with Shrimp and Mussels
Rice Noodles with Shrimp 188
  and Coconut-Lime Dressing
Jambalaya with 190
  Shrimp and Sausage
Grilled Ahi Tuna Steak 192
  with Bing Cherry Salsa
Rosemary Salmon with 194
  Caramelized Oranges
Lobster Stuffed with Crab Imperial . . . 196
Pan-Seared Salmon with 198
  Creamy Cilantro Lime Sauce
Seafood Paella 200
Pan-Seared Scallops with 202
  Lemon Caper Sauce
Caribbean White Fish 204
  in Curry Sauce
Rich and Creamy Lobster Pot Pie 206

Pastas and Pizza 209
Baked Ziti with 210
  Sausage and Peppers
Italian Sausage and 212
  Spinach Gnocchi
Creamy Cajun Chicken 214
  Alfredo with Smoked
  Sausage
Individual Pizza Pot Pies 216
Bacon Cheeseburger 218
  Lasagna

Desserts and Sweets 221
Blueberry and Lemon 222
  Bread Pudding
Apple Dumplings 224
Chocolate Raspberry Tart 226
Appeltaart: .228
  Dutch Apple Pie
Bananas Foster 230
Peanut Butter Cheesecake 232
  with Chocolate Graham
  Cracker Crust
Arroz con Dulce 234
  (Puerto Rican Rice Pudding)
Mom's Date Nut Pudding 236
Chocolate Marshmallow 238
  Bread Pudding
Individual Pineapple 240
  Upside-Down Cakes
Very Berry Pie 242

Baked Goodies 245
Banana Walnut Bread 246
Cinnamon Apple Scones 248
Blueberry-Lemon Scones 250
Mango Bread 252

Index 255

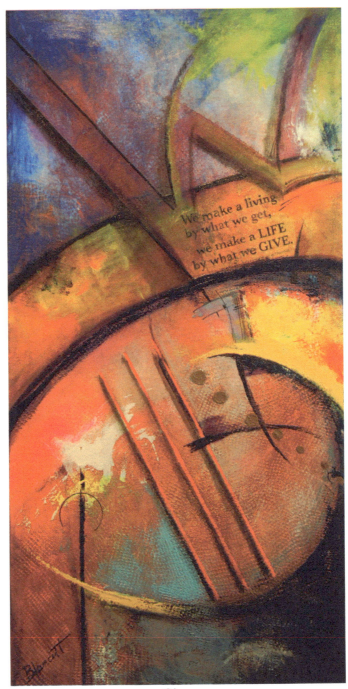

Give

Foreword by S. Alison Chabonais

National Editor, *Natural Awakenings* magazine (2004 - 2019)

"Artist in the Kitchen" embodies Stephen Blancett's lifework of creating luscious dishes that fit into people's repertoire of taste treats. As a longtime National Editor of *Natural Awakenings* magazine, I was privileged to witness his artful cookery as the National Art Director as it dominated its niche. What floored me was the extraordinary extras he freely contributed. His sole reward? The culinary enjoyment of readers.

Each month, Stephen volunteered a weekend to prepare recipes for our Conscious Eating section, challenged by our national publisher's penchant for organic, plant-based foods. Ingredients often had to be tweaked. Calling on his 30 years of experience in directing publishing and advertising industry food photography, he tapped his sizable props closet to produce inviting images that unfailingly engaged home cooks at their first glance.

"I believe that the best food tastes great and is visually tasty, too — colorful and fun — like my paintings," he says. The many skills developed in creating his internationally exhibited, museum-level paintings inform all that he does.

Stephen's love of cooking, launched at age 8 in a next-door neighbor's Greek kitchen, bloomed at age 20. That's when he bought his first cookbook and began seriously experimenting. Buffet leftovers carried home from a college job on a tourist paddleboat were his medium. He began working on transforming them into nourishment that his friends would relish.

Since then, he's explored flavorful recipes packed-in while climbing Mount Kilimanjaro, variations of traditional French and English faire, and Caribbean islands' cuisine sampled during visits that later led to a vacation home on St. Thomas. James Caudill-Ritter, his husband and official taster, has encouraged expansion into German and Puerto Rican offerings based on earlier travels. Mouth-watering adventures in foodstuffs never stop.

Today his art studio hosts over 100 cookbooks. "I like the personal touch, authors you can relate to," he says. Favorites include Jacques Pépin, Lidia Bastianich, David Venable, Martha Stewart, and of course Snoop Dogg.

"When I find a dish I love," he says, "I dissect it to make it my own." That inventive spirit now extends to an unusual set of rubs and sauces like blueberry BBQ and coconut curry.

Stephen's generous spirit colors all he does. For over 20 years, fans have purchased his annual donation of an original, larger-than-life painting to Southwest Florida's Fine Arts Auction to benefit Abuse and Counseling Treatment, Inc. He's served as the non-profit's chair, co-chair and artistic director. This year he's also gifting an artful dinner for 8 to the highest bidder. He's taught art at kids' camps and supports a local children's hospital as well as a school and clinic in Tanzania, East Africa, for which his crew raised nearly a quarter-million dollars.

This passionate man loves to entertain, whether cooking a crowd-pleasing meal for 20 coworkers at a company holiday party or 200 friends just for fun. "It's like painting for me," he says. "I'm creating something good and watching friends enjoy something I made." His first cookbook is filled with more than 100 of his favorite recipes, from appetizers to baked goodies, every one specially selected through the years, each clearly and beautifully photographed. These tried-and-true dishes easily fit into daily life as favorite mainstays and tasty splurges.

Cocktailed

Introduction

In a roundabout way, this book was inspired by Porky Pig, Bugs Bunny, Huckleberry Hound, and the Pink Panther. My creative mind was first sparked by these Saturday morning TV cartoon characters of the 1960s and '70s. While other kids watched them for the laughs, I would watch with a pen and paper in hand, so I could draw my animated heros. My passion for creating art continued to grow from that point on.

For me, cooking is another way to express my creativity. It's kind of like combining a paint palette with taste palates. I have been working on this cookbook for over 10 years. Being housebound during the COVID-19 pandemic for over a year allowed me the time to finally finish it.

The recipes in this book do not follow a specific theme; they are an assortment of some of my all-time favorites. Many were inspired by my travels while exhibiting my art around the world. You may notice some have a Caribbean twist. That comes from my 30-year-plus love affair with the U.S. Virgin Islands. My husband James and I have a second home on St. Thomas. We love the food of the islands. Other recipes are from my childhood and inspirations from many friends.

My artwork is always bright and colorful; I designed this book to be the same. A vibrant, full-page photo accompanies each recipe. I believe if you see the final product, you are more likely to make it. I have also included images of some of my paintings. I hate seeing cookbooks with little or no photography or illustrations. To me, pages of just text are dull and boring, and not very appetizing.

I grew up in Southeastern Ohio. The Nicholakis family lived in the three houses next to ours.

Sophie Nicholakis lived directly beside us. She was an elderly, widowed woman, who was immaculate in every way. Despite the differences in our ages, Sophie and I became very good friends.

We spent many summer evenings together sitting on her front porch glider, watching cars go by and chatting about current happenings, while enjoying a slice of her homemade spanakopita (spinach pie) or baklava. Some of my favorite recipes came from Sophie.

My mother enjoyed cooking and experimenting with new recipes. But, like most households of the 1970s, we also had our share of heat-and-eat TV dinners. She had a large, "well-used" cookbook from the 1940s. It was stuffed with recipes she had clipped from magazines and many handwritten ones from her friends and family members. It was her cookbook bible. She gave the book to me several years ago; it's one of my most cherished possessions.

One of my fondest childhood memories is sitting at the kitchen table watching my mother prepare holiday dinners. She would assign me an easy task, like chopping nuts or peeling potatoes. When I completed my task, she would lovely pat me on the cheek. I recall the smell of freshly chopped onions on her hands. To this day, when I chop onions, I always sniff my hands and smile. It's a "comfort smell". Mom's recipe for date nut pudding is a long-standing holiday tradition (see page 236).

I tried to make the recipes easy-to-follow, so anyone can create their own culinary masterpieces. I hope you enjoy the book and embrace and savor the flavor of each recipe.

Seashine

Acknowledgments

My dear mother, Norma Jean Hughes, died a few months prior to me finishing this book. I thank her for giving me life, nurturing me, and always being my friend. She was always the first person I would call for advice or just to say hello. There are not enough words to describe how important she was in my life; even though she is gone, she continues to influence me. I am forever grateful. As she said before she passed away, "It's been a good ride."

A huge thank you to my good friend and editor, Randy Kambic. I've had the joy of working with Randy on numerous projects for over 10 year. Thank you for your keen eye, attention to details, your patience and for the many hours you devoted to this book.

To Alison Chabonais, a supremely gifted writer. I am honored to call you my friend. I thank you for writing the foreword to this book and making me sound more than what I am.

Particular thanks go to my dear friends Drew Hagenah and Jim Richardson for the many years of friendship and for being the best men at our wedding. Drew, I am very appreciative for you graciously proofreading every recipe with spectacular speed and accuracy. Jim, thanks for your continued support, cheerleading me on this project, honest feedback and for being a good eater.

To my family and many friends and followers on social media, I am overwhelmed by your support.

Love for Lori

Appetizers

Pastry-Wrapped Baked Brie with Sautéed Plums and Shallots

Servings: 8 to 10

Ingredients
BAKED BRIE
2 tbsp unsalted butter
1 sheet frozen puff pastry, thawed
8 oz wheel brie cheese
1 tbsp fig preserves
1 egg, beaten
Coarse sugar, for sprinkling

PLUMS AND SHALLOTS
1 shallot, sliced thin
2 tbsp unsalted butter
4 plums, pitted and cut into wedges
2 tsp sugar
1 tbsp fresh ginger, grated
1 tbsp lemon juice
2 springs fresh thyme, for garnish

How to make it
PLUMS AND SHALLOTS
In a large skillet, melt butter over medium-high heat. Once melted, add the plums and shallots. Reduce heat to medium-low and sauté, stirring occasionally, for 5 minutes.

Add the sugar, ginger and lemon juice and cook, stirring occasionally, until the sugar dissolves and the plums begin to break down around the edges, about 10 or 15 minutes. Remove from heat and set aside.

BAKED BRIE
Preheat the oven to 425° F.

Lay the puff pastry flat on a parchment-lined baking sheet. Place the brie in the center. Spread the fig preserves evenly on top of the brie. Fold the 4 corners of the pastry over the brie. Brush the pastry with the beaten egg and sprinkle lightly with sugar.

Bake until golden-brown, about 25 to 30 minutes.

Use the parchment paper to transfer the brie to a serving plate. Spoon the plums and shallots over the top.

Serve warm, garnished with fresh thyme. Enjoy with sliced baguette and/or crackers.

Fried Green Tomatoes with Spicy Remoulade Sauce

Servings: 4

Ingredients

SPICY REMOULADE SAUCE
¾ cup mayonnaise
¼ cup sour cream
1 tsp hot pepper sauce
1 tsp cayenne pepper
1 tsp garlic powder
2 tsp Dijon mustard
2 tbsp sweet pickle relish
1 tsp lemon juice

FRIED GREEN TOMATOES
Canola oil for frying (or other oil with a high smoke point)
2 tsp butter
Salt for seasoning
4 large, firm, green tomatoes
½ cup flour
½ cup milk
1 large egg
1½ tsp vinegar
½ cup fine cornmeal
1 tsp garlic powder
1 tsp smoked paprika
2 tsp cayenne pepper
Salt and black pepper to taste

How to make it

SPICY REMOULADE SAUCE
I like to make the sauce first, so it has time to chill. Mix all of the sauce ingredients in a bowl until smooth. Place the bowl in the refrigerator until ready to use.

FRIED GREEN TOMATOES
Slice the tomatoes into ½-inch slices, discard the ends. Season with salt and place on a paper towel-lined plate and set aside.

Set out 3 shallow bowls. Place the flour in the first bowl. In the second bowl, whisk the milk, egg and vinegar together and in the third bowl, mix together the cornmeal, garlic powder, paprika and cayenne pepper.

Pat tomato slices dry with paper towels. Dip the tomato slices, one at a time, in the flour, coat both sides with the flour, then dip them into the milk/egg mixture; next, dredge both sides of the slices in the cornmeal mixture. Place the tomatoes on a cooling rack for 10 minutes so the coating can set.

Pour enough oil into a cast iron or stainless steel skillet to reach a depth of ¼- to ½-inch. Add the butter and heat over medium heat until very hot, but not smoking.

Use tongs to lower the coated tomatoes into the hot oil. Fry the tomatoes in batches of 4 at a time for 3-5 minutes on each side or until golden brown.

Transfer the cooked tomatoes on paper towels to drain and sprinkle them with a bit of salt and black pepper.

Serve immediately with the remoulade sauce.

NOTE: Remoulade sauce is also delectable with crab cakes, baked fish, French fries or used as a sandwich spread.

Caribbean Conch Fritters with Orange Aioli

Conch meat may be hard to find outside the Caribbean, but you can sometimes find it canned. For a good substitute, use chopped clams, chopped shrimp or crabmeat.

Servings: 4 to 6

Ingredients
ORANGE AIOLI
¾ cup mayonnaise
2 garlic cloves, minced
1 tsp grated orange rind
1 tbsp fresh orange juice
¼ tsp salt
¼ tsp white pepper

FRITTERS
Canola oil for frying (or other oil with a high smoke point)
2 cups conch meat, finely chopped
3 garlic cloves, finely minced
2 eggs, beaten
¼ cup buttermilk
1 cup all-purpose flour
1 jalapeño, seeded and finely minced
¼ cup white onion, finely minced
¼ cup red bell pepper, seeded and finely minced
2 tsp baking powder
¼ tsp cayenne pepper
Salt and pepper to taste

How to make it
ORANGE AIOLI
Mix all of the aioli ingredients in a bowl until smooth. Place the bowl in the refrigerator until ready to use. Aioli will stay good in the refrigerator for 2 to 3 days.

FRITTERS
Add the conch, onion, garlic, eggs, red bell pepper, jalapeño and buttermilk together in a large bowl. Refrigerate for at least 30 minutes to let the batter rest.

In another bowl, mix together the flour, baking powder and cayenne pepper. Stir the flour mixture into the conch mixture to form a thick batter and season with salt and pepper.

Heat about 1 inch of oil in a large cast iron or stainless steel skillet over medium heat. When the oil is hot, drop one tbsp of batter into the oil and fry until browned on one side.

Flip and brown on the other side. Place on a paper towel-lined plate to drain and repeat with the remaining batter.

Transfer the fritters to a serving dish, drizzle with the orange aioli and serve.

Shrimp Ceviche

This easy shrimp ceviche recipe requires no cooking and takes only 20 to 30 minutes to make. I love serving it with tortilla chips as an appetizer or as a topping on steaks, chicken or hamburgers.

Servings: 4 to 6

Ingredients
1 lb pre-cooked, peeled and deveined medium shrimp
¼ cup freshly squeezed lemon juice
¼ cup freshly squeezed lime juice
2 medium tomatoes, chopped
1 small red onion, finely chopped
1 jalapeño, seeded and finely chopped
½ cup fresh cilantro leaves, finely chopped
½ tsp kosher salt
½ tsp white pepper
1 Hass avocado, diced (use one that is ripe, but not too mushy)

How to make it
Remove the tails from the shrimp and chop into even bite-sized pieces and place in a large bowl.

Add the lemon juice, lime juice, tomatoes, red onion, jalapeño, cilantro, salt and white pepper, and gently toss together. Cover and refrigerate for at least 1 hour.

Just before serving, add the diced avocado and gently toss in combining.

Serve with tortilla or pita chips.

NOTE: This can also be served as a side dish or as a topping on steaks, chicken or hamburgers.

Beer-Battered Fried Pickles with Spicy Ranch Dressing

For me, beer-battered fried pickles are the ultimate guilty pleasure appetizer. This recipe is inspired by the ones served at Bernie's Bar & Grill on St. Thomas. They go great with a margarita or two (or more).

Servings: 8

Ingredients
SPICY RANCH DRESSING
1 cup mayonnaise
½ cup sour cream
1 tsp dried dill weed
1 tsp dried chives
½ tsp dried parsley
½ tsp cayenne pepper
½ tsp garlic powder
½ tsp onion powder
¼ tsp salt
¼ tsp black pepper

FRIED PICKLES
Oil for frying (grapeseed or other high smoke point oil)
1 (32 oz) jar dill or bread and butter pickle slices, drained
1 large egg
1 (12 oz) can of your favorite beer
1 tbsp baking powder
1 tsp hot sauce
¼ tsp salt
¼ tsp black pepper
1½ cups all-purpose flour

How to make it
RANCH DRESSING
In a small bowl, whisk together all of the ingredients. Cover and refrigerate for at least 30 minutes before serving.

FRIED PICKLES
Pat the pickles dry with paper towels and set aside.

In a medium bowl, whisk together the egg, beer, baking powder, hot sauce, salt and pepper. Whisk in flour.

Pour about 1½ inches of oil into a Dutch oven or a medium-sized saucepan. Heat oil to 375° F. A candy thermometer is helpful for this.

Dip the pickle slices in the batter. Using tongs, carefully place them into the hot oil, 7 to 10 at a time; fry until golden brown on both sides (about 3 to 4 minutes).

Remove with a slotted spoon and place on a paper towel-lined plate.

Serve hot with spicy ranch dressing on the side.

Spicy Black-Eyed Pea Hummus

Tip: Hummus can be made a day or two in advance and is best when served chilled.

Ingredients
3 cups black-eyed peas, cooked and drained
3 garlic cloves, chopped
¼ cup fresh lemon juice
Grated zest of 1 lemon
1 tsp chilli powder
1 medium jalapeño pepper, seeded and chopped
1 medium red bell pepper, seeded and chopped
1 tsp crushed red pepper
1 tbsp olive oil
Dash of salt and pepper

DRIZZLE
1 tbsp olive oil
Dash or two of hot sauce

TOPPING (optional)
¼ cup grated cheddar cheese

How to make it
Place ingredients in a food processor; process until smooth. Spoon hummus mixture into a medium serving bowl, spread/flatten and garnish with grated cheddar cheese. Mix 1 tbsp of olive oil with a dash or two of your favorite hot sauce and drizzle over the hummus and cheese. Serve with pita wedges or your favorite crackers.

Who Dat

Breakfast and Brunch

Hawaiian Pancakes

Makes: 12 to 14 pancakes

Ingredients
2 cups oatmeal pancake mix
   (you can use wheat based, but
   the oatmeal is healthier for
   your heart)
1 cup of fresh pineapple (skinned,
   cored and finely chopped)
¼ cup grated fresh coconut
1 can (15 oz) of cream of coconut
3 large eggs
1 tsp vanilla extract

Tip: Too much juice from the pineapple will make the batter too runny. Drain juice from the pineapple and pat with paper towels.

TOPPING
1 cup vanilla yogurt
Maple syrup
Your favorite fruit: blueberries, strawberries,
   pineapple, mango or papaya

How to make it
In a large mixing bowl, combine the pancake mix, cream of coconut, eggs and vanilla. Stir with a wire whisk until smooth, also stir in the chopped pineapple and coconut. Let stand 2 to 3 minutes.

Heat nonstick, electric griddle to 350° F or use a skillet over medium heat, lightly coated with cooking spray or vegetable oil. Pour about a ¼ cup of batter for each pancake into skillet. Cook the pancakes until little bubbles start to form and bottoms are lightly browned; flip and brown the other side.

Arrange four or five pancakes on a plate, top with fruit, drizzle with maple syrup and one or two teaspoons of vanilla yogurt.

Bacon-Kale Egg Breakfast Muffins with Sun-Dried Tomatoes

These yummy egg muffins are basically mini-frittatas. I like to make them ahead, chill them in the refrigerator and when I'm ready for an easy morning breakfast, I just pop them in the microwave for about 30-45 seconds.

Servings: 12 muffins

Ingredients
1 tbsp olive oil
1 medium onion, finely chopped
3 cloves garlic, minced
7 to 9 slices precooked bacon, chopped
1 (3-oz package) sun-dried tomatoes, finely chopped
2 cups kale, chopped
10 eggs
½ tsp paprika
½ tsp salt
½ tsp freshly ground black pepper
1 (8-oz package) cheddar cheese, shredded

How to make it
Preheat oven to 350° F.

Heat olive oil in a large pan or skillet over medium-high heat until shimmering. Add the onion and sauté for 3 to 4 minutes. Add the garlic and sauté for one additional minute.

Add sun-dried tomatoes and kale, and cook for 4 to 5 minutes, until the kale wilts. Turn off heat and set aside.

In a meduim-size mixing bowl, whisk the eggs, paprika, and salt and pepper. Fold in cooked vegetable mixture, bacon and cheddar cheese, mix until well combined.

Spray the muffin pan with baking spray, then pour an equal amount of mixture into each cup, filling to just below the rim.

Bake until cooked through and golden, 30 to 35 minutes.

Enjoy while hot, or cool and refrigerate in an airtight container until ready to eat.

Eggs Benedict with Prosciutto

I love trying variations of eggs benedict when I travel. This recipe is inspired from one of my favorite hotels, the Hari, located in the Belgravia district in central London. I like to serve it with asparagus or sliced avocado.

Servings: 4

Ingredients
EGGS BENEDICT
4 large eggs
8 cups water
2 tbsp white vinegar
4 English muffins, split in half
8 slices prosciutto
¼ cup fresh chives, chopped

HOLLANDAISE SAUCE
4 egg yolks
2 tbsp lemon juice
1 tsp Dijon mustard
¼ tsp salt
½ tsp smoked paprika
½ cup butter, melted

How to make it
EGGS BENEDICT
In a large pot, bring the water and vinegar to a low boil; reduce to low. Crack the eggs into individual ramekins or small bowls. Hold the ramekin close to the water's surface and carefully slip the egg into the water.

Cook the eggs for 5 minutes or until whites and yolks are firm and not runny. Carefully remove the eggs with a slotted spoon and place on a plate topped with a paper towel.

While the eggs are cooking, split the English muffins in half, toast them and set aside.

HOLLANDAISE SAUCE
Add the egg yolks, lemon juice, Dijon mustard, salt and smoked paprika to a blender. Process on high speed until slightly thickened and pale yellow.

Reduce blender speed to low; in a slow steady stream, add melted butter to yolk mixture.

Return blender to high speed and process until thickened, around 30-40 seconds. Keep the sauce warm until serving by placing the blender container in a pan of hot water.

If necessary, thin the Hollandaise sauce with a tablespoon or 2 of warm water.

Top each English muffin half with 2 slices of prosciutto and a poached egg. Spoon Hollandaise sauce over the poached eggs, sprinkle with chopped chives and serve immediately.

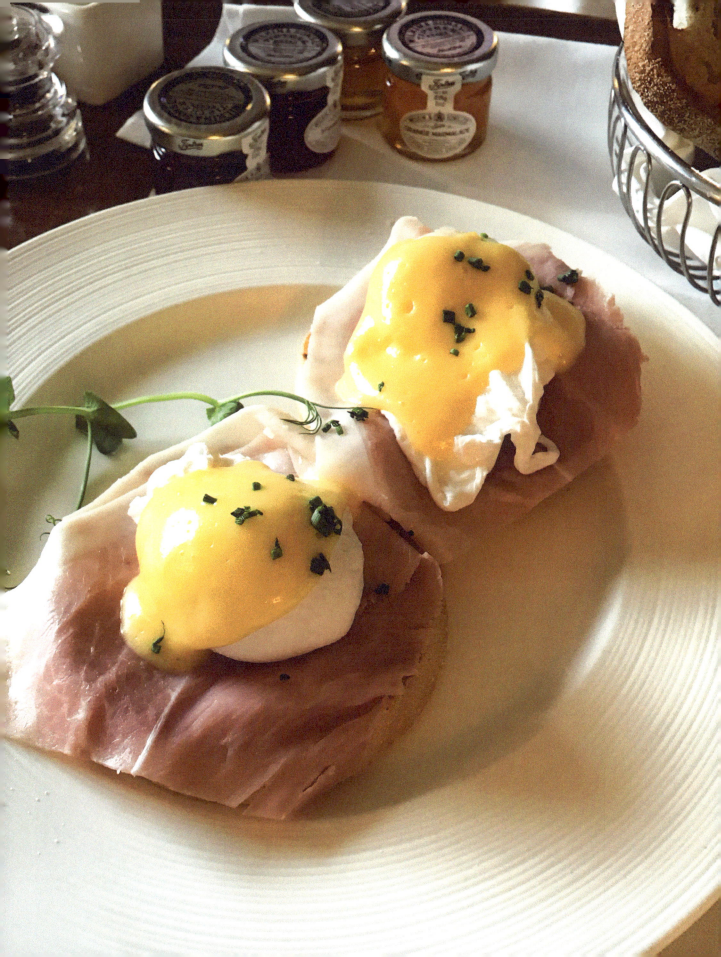

Smoked Salmon Eggs Benedict with Pan-Seared Tomatoes and Asparagus

Servings: 2

Ingredients
EGGS BENEDICT
4 tsp olive oil, divided
2 large, firm, ripe tomatoes, cut into 4 thick slices
1 tsp salt
½ tsp freshly ground black pepper
2 tbsp fresh dill, chopped, plus more for garnish
16 asparagus spears, with the woody ends cut off
1 red onion, sliced thin
4 large eggs
8 cups water
2 tbsp white vinegar
4 oz smoked salmon
1 tbsp capers
¼ tsp paprika

HOLLANDAISE SAUCE
4 large egg yolks
1 tsp Dijon mustard
1 tbsp fresh lemon juice
1 tsp salt
1 tsp freshly ground black pepper
½ cup butter, melted

How to make it
EGGS BENEDICT
Heat 2 tsp olive oil in a grill pan or large heavy skillet over medium-high heat. Add the tomato slices and cook for 4 minutes on each side. Transfer the cooked tomatoes to a plate and sprinkle with the chopped dill, salt and pepper and set aside.

Using the same pan, add the remaining 2 tsp of olive oil. Use tongs to place the asparagus in the pan. Cook for 6 to 8 minutes turning frequently. Transfer the cooked asparagus to a plate and set aside.

HOLLANDAISE SAUCE
Place the egg yolks, mustard, lemon juice, salt and pepper into a blender and blend until combined. With the blender running, slowly pour in the melted butter and allow the sauce to emulsify. If the Hollandaise sauce becomes too thick, add a tablespoon or 2 of hot water.

Poach the eggs last. In a large pot, bring the water and vinegar to a low boil. Crack the eggs into individual ramekins or small bowls. Hold the ramekin close to the water's surface and carefully slip the egg into the water.

Cook the eggs for 5 minutes or until whites and yolks are firm and not runny. Carefully remove the eggs with a slotted spoon and place on a plate topped with a paper towel.

To assemble, first layer each tomato slice with 4 asparagus spears, top with red onion slices, follow with smoked salmon and poached egg, and a generous amount of Hollandaise.

Garnish with fresh dill, capers, red onion slices and a light sprinkle of paprika.

Dutch Baby Pancake with Blackberries and Sliced Almonds

I love making this classic recipe for breakfast whenever we have company staying at our home. Although this recipe calls for blackberries and almonds, you can use any kind of berry. I've even made it with pineapple and coconut.

Servings: 4

Ingredients
4 tbsp unsalted butter, melted
4 large eggs
½ cup milk
½ cup all-purpose flour
2 tbsp granulated sugar
¼ tsp salt
2 tsp pure vanilla extract
¼ cup confectioners' sugar
1 cup blackberries
½ cup sliced almonds

How to make it
In a blender or a food processor, blend together eggs, milk, flour, sugar, salt and vanilla until a thin batter forms, about one minute. Let the batter rest in the blender.

Place a 12-inch cast iron or other oven-proof skillet with 4 tbsp butter in the oven.

With the skillet in the oven, preheat oven to 425° F.

When the oven has preheated, carefully remove pan, swirl butter around to coat skillet, and pour in the batter.

Return to the oven and bake until pancake is puffy and golden, about 20 to 25 minutes.

Remove from oven and arrange the blackberries and sliced almonds on top and dust with powdered sugar.

Serve while hot from skillet or transfer to a plate.

Ham and Cheese Casserole with Hash Brown Crust

Servings: 8

Ingredients
HASH BROWN CRUST
16-oz package frozen hash browns, thawed
2 tbsp butter, melted
2 eggs
1 tsp oregano
1 tsp onion powder
1 tsp garlic powder
½ tsp salt
1 tsp black pepper

CASSEROLE
2½ cups milk
6 eggs, lightly beaten
1 cup all-purpose flour
1½ tsp baking powder
2 cups cooked ham, diced
10 oz frozen broccoli, chopped
1 small yellow onion, chopped
2 cups sharp cheddar cheese, shredded
1 tsp salt
1 tsp black pepper

How to make it
Preheat oven to 400° F.

Line a 9-inch springform pan with parchment paper, including the sides. Apply baking spray on top of the parchment paper.

Note: If you are using a non-leak springform pan, you don't need to use parchment paper.

For a firm and crispy crust, the hash browns need to be as dry as possible. Squeeze out as much excess moisture from hash browns as you can and then pat with paper towel.

In a large bowl, mix the dried hash browns, butter, eggs, oregano, onion powder, garlic powder, salt and pepper. Press hash brown mixture onto bottom and up the sides of the prepared springform pan. Press firmly against the bottom and edges.

Place on a rimmed baking sheet and bake for 20-25 minutes or until the hash browns start to crisp and turn brown. Remove from oven and set aside.

Meanwhile, in a large bowl, whisk together the milk and eggs, then add the flour and baking powder, ham, broccoli, onions, cheddar cheese, salt and pepper, and stir until well combined. Pour into the hash brown crust pan.

Reduce the heat to 350° F and bake for 45 to 50 minutes. Allow to cool slightly before unlocking the spring form pan. Remove from the pan and peel off the parchment paper before serving. Cut into slices for serving.

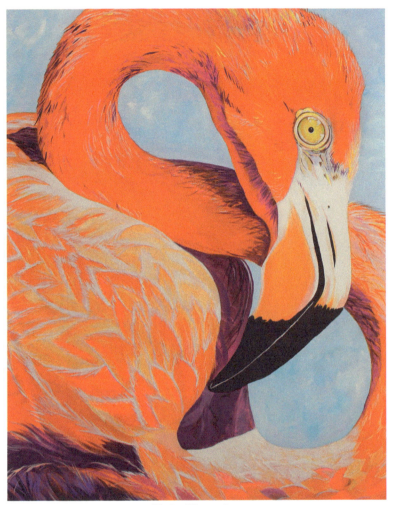

Bird of Paradise

Soups, Stews and Chili

Caribbean Beef Pepperpot Stew

Pepper pot stew is a very common dish in Jamaica and other islands in the Caribbean. I originally learned to make this recipe from a Cuban friend of mine years ago. I have tweaked it over the years to my own personal taste. I hope you love these fantastic, complex flavors as much as I do.

Servings: 4 to 6

Ingredients
2 tsp olive oil
1 lb lean stewing beef, cut into bite-size pieces
2 red peppers, seeded and cut into bite-size pieces
1 sweet potato, peeled and cut into bite-size pieces
12 oz fresh green beans, trimmed and halved
2 garlic cloves, minced
2 tbsp jerk seasoning
1 tbsp white vinegar
1 tsp sugar
14.5 oz tomato purée
1 small onion, finely chopped
8 oz beef stock
2 tbsp Worcestershire sauce
½ tsp salt
½ tsp freshly ground black pepper
2 cups long-grain white rice

How to make it
In a large skillet, heat olive oil over medium heat. Add the beef and cook for 4-5 minutes, or until lightly browned, stirring occasionally.

Add the red peppers, sweet potato, beans, garlic, jerk seasoning, white vinegar, sugar, tomato purée, onion, beef stock and Worcestershire sauce. Season with salt and pepper and stir well.

Reduce heat to low, cover and simmer for 1 to 1½ hours, or until the beef is tender.

Cook the rice according to the package instructions.

Serve the stew hot over rice.

Spicy African Chicken Peanut Stew

Peanut stew is a staple of African cuisine. There are endless variations of recipes for it. The first time I tried it was while climbing Mount Kilimanjaro. Our chef cooked it in a large pot over an open fire. It was absolutely delicious! If you are not a fan of hot chiles, skip or reduce the amount of cayenne pepper.

Servings: 6 to 8

Ingredients
2 lb boneless chicken breast, cut into bite-size cubes
1 to 2 tbsp olive oil as needed
1 large yellow or white onion, chopped
2 tsp garlic, minced
1 tbsp grated fresh ginger or ginger paste
2-3 lb sweet potatoes, peeled and cut into bite-size cubes
½ cup creamy peanut butter
2 (14 oz) cans diced tomatoes
2 tsp smoked paprika
½ tsp ground coriander
½ tsp ground turmeric
1 tsp ground cayenne pepper
1 tsp salt
½ tsp black pepper
2 cups chicken broth
1 (14 oz) can coconut milk
2 cups spinach leaves, chopped

GARNISH
½ cup cilantro, chopped
½ cup peanuts, roughly chopped

How to make it
Heat the olive oil in a Dutch oven or large, heavy pot over medium heat. Add chicken pieces in a single layer without crowding. Cook for about 7 to 8 minutes per side or until chicken is browned; remove with tongs, and set aside on a plate. Repeat with remaining chicken pieces.

In the same pot, add the onion, garlic and ginger, and cook for 5 minutes over medium heat until the onion start to soften. Then add the sweet potatoes and peanut butter, and mix together and cook for another 5 minutes.

Add the diced tomatoes and stir until well mixed. The add the paprika, coriander, turmeric, cayenne pepper, salt and black pepper. Pour in the chicken broth and the coconut milk, stir and cook for an additional 2-3 minutes.

Return the cooked chicken along with the chopped spinach to the pot. Stir and bring to a low boil, turn down to a low simmer, cover with lid and cook for 1 hour, stirring every so often.

Turn off the heat and serve with rice, and garnish with cilantro and chopped peanuts.

U.S. Senate Bean Soup

A version of this hearty, all-American soup has been on the menu in the U.S. Senate dining room since the early 1900s. I like to serve it with homemade cornbread.

Servings: 8

Ingredients
1 lb dried Great Northern beans
2 qts chicken broth
16 oz diced smoked ham
4 tbsp butter
2 large onions, chopped
4 celery stalks, chopped
4 garlic cloves, minced
2 bay leaves
½ cup parsley, chopped
1 cup instant mashed potato flakes
Salt and freshly ground pepper

How to make it
Rinse and sort beans, then put them in a large pot or bowl, cover them with water and soak overnight. Doing this reduces the cooking time and removes some of the excess starch. You'll also have fewer split-open or burst beans.

Drain the beans.

In a Dutch oven or large pot, combine the chicken stock, the drained beans and the diced ham. Bring to a boil, then reduce heat to a low simmer.

Cover and simmer, for 2 hours; stir occasionally and skim off any froth that forms on the surface.

In a separate saucepan, heat the butter over medium heat.

Add the onions, celery and garlic, and cook for 3 to 5 minutes or until the onions are slightly translucent.

Add the onion mixture, chopped parsley and the potato flakes to the soup and simmer for an additional hour or until the beans are tender. Stir occasionally and watch to make sure that it's not burning on the bottom.

Remove bay leaves. If necessary, add more chicken stock or water to the soup to adjust the thickness.

Season to taste with salt and freshly ground pepper.

French Onion Soup

Servings: 4

Ingredients
SOUP
4 tbsp unsalted butter
2 tbsp olive oil
5 cups sliced yellow onions
   (5 to 6 medium onions)
1 tsp sugar
32 oz beef broth
¼ cup water
¼ cup dry white wine
2 tbsp Dijon mustard
2 tbsp ground thyme
1 bay leaf

TOPPINGS
1 small baguette or French bread
Unsalted butter
1 cup grated Swiss cheese
1 cup grated Gruyere cheese

Optional garnish
Fresh thyme or chives

How to make it
In a medium saucepan or Dutch oven on medium heat, melt the butter and olive oil, then add the onions and sugar, and cook until soft and caramelized—about 30 to 45 minutes. Stir often and watch not to burn.

Once the onions are caramelized, add the broth, water, wine, Dijon mustard, thyme and bay leaf.

Increase heat to high and bring to a boil, then reduce the heat to low and simmer, covered, for about 30 to 40 minutes.

Set your oven to broil. While the soup is simmering, prepare the cheese and bread. Shred the cheese and set aside. Cut the bread into ½-inch slices and butter each side, place on a cookie sheet and toast for 2 to 3 minutes per side. Once they are toasted, remove and set aside.

Once the soup has cooked, remove the bay leaf. Pour the soup into 4 individual, oven-safe bowls. Add toasted bread slices to the top of the soup; 3 to 4 should cover the top. Sprinkle on the Swiss and Gruyere cheeses.

Place the bowls on a cookie sheet and broil until the cheese has melted and has slightly browned (about 3 to 5 minutes).

Optional: Garnish with fresh thyme or chives.

Serve hot and enjoy!

Creamy Potato Mushroom Soup

Servings: 6 to 8

Ingredients
2 cups russet potatoes, peeled
  and cut into small cubes
3 celery ribs, chopped
1 garlic clove minced
1 leek (use the white parts only), chopped
1 medium yellow onion, chopped
3 tbsp olive oil
3 tbsp all-purpose flour
2 tbsp butter
8 cups vegetable stock
½ tsp salt
1 tsp pepper
¼ cup heavy cream
2 oz dried Porcini mushrooms, chopped
  and steeped in ½ cup of warm water
6 oz fresh whole Shiitake mushrooms

Optional garnish
Chopped parsley or basil

How to make it
Heat the olive oil in a 5-quart heavy pot over medium heat, add the potatoes and celery, saute for about 5 minutes then add the garlic and the leek and yellow onions and stir occasionally, until softened but not browned, about 15 minutes. Slowly add the flour until it's absorbed in the olive oil and liquid; stir to ensure there are no lumps. Cook for 1-2 minutes.

Add the vegetable stock, salt and pepper and simmer, uncovered, until vegetables are very tender, about 30 minutes.

Purée the soup in batches in a blender until smooth, then return it to the pot.

Add the Porcini mushrooms with the ½ cup of steepwater and stir in the heavy cream. Reheat the soup over low heat, stirring occasionally, about 5 to 10 minutes.

While the soup is reheating, melt the butter in a heavy skillet over moderately high heat, add the Shiitake mushrooms and sauté until golden brown, about 3 minutes.

Serve the soup topped with sautéed Shiitake mushrooms and optional chopped parsley or basil.

Asparagus Bisque

Servings: 6

Ingredients
3 tbsp olive oil
1 yellow onion, diced
2 gloves garlic, minced
2 large shallots, diced
2 celery stalks, diced
1 tsp salt
½ tsp white pepper
1 tsp fresh thyme, chopped
2 medium russet potatoes, peeled
   and diced into small cubes
4 cup chicken broth
2 lbs asparagus, cut into 1-inch pieces
   (save a few tips for garnish)
2 cups baby spinach leaves
Juice of 1 lemon
1 tbsp unsalted butter
3 tbsp sour cream, room temperature
Croutons, hot sauce, parmesan cheese,
   grated (optional garnish)

How to make it
Heat the olive oil in a Dutch oven or a large soup pot on medium-hgh heat. Add the onions, garlic, shallots, celery and salt and white pepper. Sauté until onions are soft and translucent, about 5 minutes. Add thyme and potato and sauté for another 5 minutes.

Add chicken broth and bring to a low boil. Add the asparagus, reduce heat, cover, and simmer gently for about 15 to 20 minutes, until the diced potatoes are soft and begin to break down.

Remove from heat, add the baby spinach and stir in lemon juice.

Allow the soup to cool slightly before puréeing. Using a hand immersion blender or a regular blender (if using a regular blender, work in batches), puree until silky smooth.

Add the butter to a small skillet and heat over medium-low heat. Add reserved asparagus tips and sauté for about 2 minutes, until crisp-tender.

Transfer soup to bowls, add a ½ tbsp drop of sour cream, top with croutons, asparagus tips and drizzle a little hot sauce, if desired.

Caribbean Coconut-Curry Sweet Potato Soup

Servings: 8

Ingredients
2 tbsp olive oil
1 large white onion, chopped
4 cloves garlic, chopped
2 tbsp fresh ginger, finely chopped
4 cups chicken stock
2 lbs sweet potatoes, peeled and cubed
1 tsp cayenne pepper
1 tbsp yellow curry powder
½ tsp turmeric
2 tsp brown sugar
14-oz can coconut milk
Zest and juice from 2 lemons
1 tsp white pepper
½ tsp salt
¼ cup toasted, sliced almonds for garnish

How to make it
Heat the olive oil in a Dutch oven or large, heavy pot over medium heat, add the onions and sauté for 2 minutes. Add garlic and ginger, cook for 5 minutes. Pour in the chicken stock and bring to a boil; add the cubed sweet potatoes. Reduce heat to low, cover and simmer until the sweet potatoes are very tender, about 15 to 20 minutes.

Add the cayenne pepper, curry, turmeric and brown sugar, stir until well combined and cook for 5 more minutes. Remove from the heat and let cool for 10 minutes.

Purée the soup in batches in a blender until smooth, then return to the pot. Stir in the coconut milk, lemon zest and juice. Season with white pepper and salt.

Add more stock or water if the soup seems too thick. I like it a little thick.

Pour into individual bowls and garnish with toasted almonds.

Creamy and Cheesy Sausage Potato Soup

This hearty, cheesy, creamy soup pairs perfectly with a side salad and Italian bread.

Servings: 8

Ingredients
1 tbsp olive oil
1 lb mild Italian sausage
4 cups russet potatoes, chopped
15 oz mixed frozen vegetables
   or frozen soup vegetables
4 cups chicken broth
2 cloves garlic, minced
1 tsp dried basil,
1 tsp dried parsley flakes
1 tsp salt
½ tsp black pepper
4 tbsp unsalted butter
¼ cup all-purpose flour
3 cups milk
½ cup heavy cream
2 cups colby jack cheese, shredded
¼ cup sour cream

How to make it
Heat oil in a large skillet over medium heat, add sausage and cook until no longer pink. Remove sausage with a slotted spoon and drain excess drippings from pot.

In a Dutch oven, combine the potatoes, frozen vegetables, chicken broth, garlic, basil, parsley, salt and pepper. Bring to a boil. Reduce heat; cover and simmer for 10-15 minutes or until potatoes are tender.

Meanwhile, in the skillet used to brown the sausage, melt the butter over medium heat. Stir in flour and cook, whisking constantly, for 1 minute. Slowly pour in the milk, while whisking vigorously (whisk well until smooth). Cook, stirring constantly, until mixture begins to gently boil and thicken. Stir in the heavy cream and remove from heat.

Pour the cream mixture into the soup and stir. Stir in the colby jack cheese and continue to heat until cheese is melted. Stir in sour cream and add the sausage into the soup. Taste and, if needed, add a little salt and pepper.

Serve warm with some Italian bread.

Avgolemono
(Greek Lemon Chicken Soup)

Servings: 6

Ingredients
2 tbsp olive oil
2 large boneless, skinless, chicken breasts
1 medium or large sweet onion, chopped
2 medium carrots, diced small
2 cloves garlic, minced
8 cups chicken broth
1 bay leaf
1 tsp salt
1 tsp white pepper
¾ cup Arborio rice
3 eggs
½ cup heavy cream
¼ cup fresh dill weed, chopped
Zest from 1 lemon
Juice from 2 lemons

How to make it
Heat oil in a large Dutch oven, over medium-high. Add the onion, carrots and sauté for 5 minutes, until the onions are translucent. Add garlic and sauté for 1 minute.

Add chicken broth, bay leaf, salt, white pepper and the chicken. Bring to boil, cover and reduce heat to medium-low and simmer for 20 minutes.

Remove the chicken from the pot and place on a cutting board, let cool slightly, then shred into bite-sized pieces.

Return the chicken to the pot, add the rice, cover and simmer 20 more minutes.

In a medium-size bowl, whisk together the eggs, cream and lemon zest and juice. Slowly pour the egg and cream mixture into the pot and stir until evenly combined.

Remove the bay leaf and discard. Stir in the dill weed and cook for 5 minutes. Taste and add more lemon juice, if needed. If it's too lemony, add more cream.

Garnish with lemon slices and fresh dill weed or chopped parsley.

Flying Rain

SALADS

German Roasted Purple Potato Salad

Accompany your main dish with this colorful and delicious potato salad. It's also great for summertime picnics and potluck dinners. It's good served warm or cold.

Servings: 8 to 10

Ingredients
3 lb purple potatoes, diced into medium chunks
1 red onion, diced
1 yellow bell pepper, seeded and diced into medium chunks
1 orange bell pepper, seeded and diced into medium chunks
3 tbsp olive oil
1 tsp salt
1 freshly ground pepper
8 slices of bacon, cooked and crumbled
¼ cup cider vinegar
¼ cup whole-grain mustard
2 tbsp sugar
4 green onions, sliced

How to make it
Preheat oven to 425° F.

Toss potatoes, onion and bell peppers in a large bowl with oil, salt and pepper. Transfer to a parchment paper baking sheet.

Place into the oven and roast for 25 to 35 minutes or until the potatoes are tender and cooked through, stir the potatoes every 10 or 15 minutes.

While the potatoes and peppers are roasting, cook the bacon in a skillet over medium heat, until crispy and cooked through. Transfer to a paper towel-lined plate.

Add onion, vinegar and mustard to the pan. Cook, stirring constantly and scraping up the browned bits, for 1 minute. Remove from heat.

Remove the potatoes and peppers from the oven and place into a bowl. Crumble the bacon and add it to the bowl. Drizzle the vinegar mixture on top and mix until evenly coated.

If needed, season with additional salt and pepper to taste.

Garnish with green onion slices and serve.

Sweet and Sour Three-Bean Salad

You can never have too many side dish recipes, especially one as colorful and yummy as this summertime classic.

Servings: 8 to 10

Ingredients
1 14.5-oz can green beans
1 14.5-oz can kidney beans
1 14.5-oz can wax beans
1 15-oz can chickpeas
1 medium red onion, sliced thinly
1 medium red pepper bell, chopped
½ tsp salt
½ tsp black pepper
⅔ cup vinegar
¾ cup sugar
⅓ cup oil (olive or vegetable)

How to make it
Drain and rinse beans and chickpeas, and place in a large mixing bowl; add the onions, salt and pepper, and stir.

In a small bowl, combine the vinegar, sugar and oil until sugar dissolves. Pour mixture over the beans, gently stir and refrigerate for at least 2 hours. It's best served the day after being put in the frig.

Tomato Carpaccio with Honey Dijon Vinaigrette

Servings: 4

Ingredients
3 or 4 large ripe tomatoes
1 shallot, minced
2 tsp fresh parsley, chopped
Salt and black pepper to taste
½ cup mozzarella pearls or balls
¼ cup fresh basil chiffonade

HONEY DIJON VINAIGRETTE
Ingredients
2 tbsp Dijon mustard
4 tbsp apple cider vinegar
½ tsp lemon juice
2 tsp honey
½ cup olive oil

How to make it
Core the tomatoes and slice crosswise, about ½-inch thick.

Arrange the slices overlapping on a large plate. Sprinkle the shallot, parsley, salt, pepper and mozzarella over the tomatoes.

Combine the mustard, vinegar, lemon juice, honey, salt and pepper together in a bowl. While whisking together, slowly add the olive oil.

Drizzle the dressing over the top and garnish with fresh basil chiffonade.

Spring Greens Salad with Pecan-Crusted Tofu and Mojito Dressing

Servings: 4

Ingredients

PECAN-CRUSTED TOFU
1 16-oz package firm tofu
¼ cup extra-virgin olive oil
¼ cup pecans, chopped fine or ground in food processor
¼ tsp nutmeg
Dash of salt and pepper

SALAD
10 oz mixed spring green lettuces
1 green bell pepper, seeded and cut in long, thin slices
½ English cucumber, cut into thin slices

MOJITO DRESSING
1 tsp finely grated lime zest
Juice from two limes
¼ cup chopped fresh mint
¼ cup extra-virgin olive oil
¼ cup white balsamic vinegar
2 tbsp honey
1 tbsp rum (optional)
1 tsp crushed red pepper
4 cloves garlic, chopped or minced
Dash of salt and pepper

How to make it

In a small bowl, whisk all of the ingredients for the Mojito dressing. Place in refrigerator for at least one hour before serving.

In a shallow bowl, mix pecans, nutmeg and salt and pepper.

Cut tofu width-wise into ½-inch-thick "filet" slices. Lightly brush both sides with extra-virgin olive oil. Place the tofu filets into the bowl of the pecan mixture and coat each side with the mixture.

Heat the remaining olive oil in frying pan. Fry the tofu filets until light brown, about 2 minutes each side. Let cool on paper towel, then cut into bite-size pieces.

Tip: If you have an electric grill, you could use it instead of frying.

On four individual plates, arrange lettuces, bell pepper and cucumber slices, top with pecan-crusted tofu and drizzle with Mojito dressing.

Wasabi Honey Coleslaw

This sweet-savory coleslaw with a bite of wasabi is as colorful as it is delicious. The dressing is also awesome on green salads or used as a marinade for pork or chicken.

Servings: 6 to 8

Ingredients
4 cups red cabbage, shredded
2 cups carrots, shredded
4 green oinions, both green and white parts, finely sliced
1 jalapeño, seeded and finely chopped
¼ cup fresh parsley, chopped

DRESSING
¾ cup apple cider vinegar
1 tbsp wasabi powder
1 tsp white pepper
1 tbsp yellow mustard
2 tbsp mayonnaise
1 tbsp fresh lime juice
¼ cup honey
1 tsp black sesame seeds
1 tsp white sesame seeds

How to make it
In a large bowl, combine the cabbage, carrots, green onions, jalapeño and parsley.

In a small bowl, whisk the vinegar, wasabi powder, white pepper, mustard, mayonnaise, lime juice and honey.

Pour dressing over the cabbage mixture and toss lightly until well-blended. Serve immediately or cover and chill in refrigerator for a few hours or overnight.

Garnish with a light sprinkle of black and white sesame seeds and serve.

Roasted Beet Salad with Apples, Feta and Candied Walnuts

Servings: 6

Ingredients

DRESSING
¼ cup balsamic vinegar
¾ cup olive oil
2 tbsp honey
1 tbsp Dijon mustard
½ tsp dried basil
½ tsp salt
½ tsp freshly ground black pepper
1 garlic clove, minced

CANDIED WALNUTS
1 tbsp butter
¼ cup granulated sugar
1 cup walnuts, roughly chopped

BEETS
2 bunches of small to medium fresh beets (about 6-8 beets)
2 tbsp olive oil
½ tsp salt
½ tsp freshly ground black pepper

SALAD
1½ cup baby spinach
2 Granny Smith apples, cores removed and thinly sliced
½ cup feta cheese, crumbled

How to make it

DRESSING
Place all of the dressing ingredients in a mixing bowl. Whisk together until thoroughly combined. Place in the refrigerator until ready to serve.

CANDIED WALNUTS
Melt the butter in a small, non-stick skillet over medium heat. Add sugar and stir lightly until the sugar has mostly melted. When it starts bubbling, add the walnuts and stir until well coated, then transfer them to a sheet pan lined with parchment paper to cool.

BEETS
Arrange a rack in the middle of the oven and preheat to 425° F.

Cut off the stems and clean beets thoroughly and pat dry with paper towels. Slice in half with a sharp knife. Place the beets on a sheet of aluminum foil, drizzle with olive oil and season with salt and pepper before wrapping in the foil. Place on a rimmed baking sheet.

Roast for 50 to 60 minutes. They are done when a thin knife or fork slides easily to the center of the beets. Remove from the oven and let cool for at least an hour.

Once the beets have cooled, remove the skins by holding one of the beets in a paper towel and use the edges of the paper to rub the skin away. Cut the beets into ½-inch wedges.

BUILD THE SALAD
Arrange a bed of spinach onto a large platter, top with the roasted beets, sliced apples, candied walnuts and crumbled feta cheese, and lightly toss. Give the chilled dressing a final whisk and pour over the salad.

Bloody Mary Shrimp and Pasta Salad

Servings: 8 to 10

Ingredients
DRESSING
½ cup olive oil
¼ cup red wine vinegar
6 oz tomato paste
¼ cup vodka
3 tbsp Worcestershire sauce
1 tbsp horseradish
1 garlic clove, minced
2 tsp hot sauce
1 tsp salt
2 tsp black pepper

SALAD
16 oz cavatappi pasta, cooked and drained
1 pt cherry or grape tomatoes, halved
1 cup celery, sliced
1 cup cooked bacon, crumbled
1 green bell pepper, seeded and cut into ½ inch squares
1 red bell pepper, seeded and cut into ½ inch squares
2 medium red onions, chopped
¾ cup green, pimento-stuffed olives, sliced in half
8 oz mozzarella, cubed
12 to 16 jumbo shrimp, cooked, peeled and deveined with tails on

How to make it
In a medium bowl, whisk together the olive oil, red wine vinegar, tomato paste, vodka, Worcestershire sauce, horseradish, garlic, hot sauce, salt and black pepper.

In a large bowl, add cooked cavatappi pasta, tomatoes, celery, bacon, green and red bell peppers, red onion, olives and mozzarella.

Pour dressing over salad, toss together until evenly combined.

Cover the bowl with cling wrap, and refrigerate for 2 hours or overnight.

Remove the pasta from the fridge and give the pasta salad a generous stir.

Arrange the shrimp around the rim of the bowl and serve.

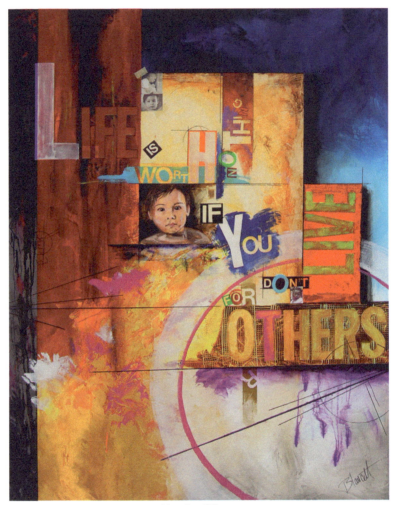

Live For Others

Vegetables and Side Dishes

Baked Mashed Potatoes

Servings: 6

Ingredients
4 lbs Yukon Gold potatoes (peeled and chopped into quarters)
3 cloves garlic, minced
1 cup sour cream
4 oz cream cheese
¼ cup chives, chopped
3 tbsp unsalted butter, melted
10 slices of bacon, cooked, drained and crumbled
1 cup shredded cheddar cheese
¼ to ½ cup milk
Salt and pepper to taste

How to make it
Preheat oven to 350° F.

In a large pot of boiling water, cook potatoes until they are fork tender (about 20 to 30 minutes), drain well.

Drain and return the potatoes back to the pot, add the garlic, sour cream, cream cheese, garlic powder, chives, bacon and ¾ cup of the cheddar cheese.

Using a hand mixer, slowly add the milk and mix/mash until the potatoes are the consistency you'd like. Add salt and pepper to taste.

Place mashed potatoes in an 9"x13" baking dish. Top with remaining cheddar cheese and drizzle with butter.

Place in oven uncovered and bake for 30 minutes.

Let sit for 10 to 15 minutes before serving.

Optional: I like to sprinkle the top with a little more pepper and chives before serving.

Mofongo
(Puerto Rican-Style Plantains)

The ingredients of this traditional Puerto Rican dish are normally mashed with a mortar and pestle, but I find it easier to use a food processor. It is often served as a side dish to pork, beef, chicken or seafood. It can also be served in a bowl with a little chicken stock or soup.

Servings: 4

Ingredients
- 4 green (unripe) plantains, peeled and cut into ½ inch slices
- 1 cup pork cracklings (pork rinds)
- 1 slice bacon, cooked and crumbled
- 3 to 5 garlic cloves, minced
- 4 tsp of olive oil
- ½ tsp kosher salt
- 3 tsp chicken or beef broth
- 2 cups frying oil

How to make it

Heat frying oil in a large pot or Dutch oven over medium heat. Fry plaintain slices in small batches for about 10 to 12 minutes or until they turn a light golden brown. Make sure to turn plantains as they cook.

Remove from oil and place on paper towels to drain.

Place the fried plantains and the remaining ingredients into a food processor, do this in batches if necessary. Pulse until mixture starts to form a ball. Make sure everything is well mixed, but not smooth. You'll want it to be a little chunky.

Use four small ramekins as molds. Spray the ramekins with cooking spray and spoon-in the mofongo and pack firmly. Loosen the edges with a knife and flip onto a plate, slowly lift and remove the ramekins and serve.

Mofongo is best served immediately, as it can fall apart quickly.

Festive Fondant Potatoes

The recipe for fondant potatoes originated in France. They are also referred to as melting potatoes.

Searing the potatoes ensures a crunchy outside and roasting them in buttery chicken broth with garlic and herbs allows the potatoes to absorb the liquid, making the insides moist and flavorful.

Servings: 4

Ingredients
4 large russet potatoes
2 tsp vegetable oil
4 tsp butter (cut into small pieces)
2 cloves garlic (minced)
4 sprigs fresh thyme
4 sprigs fresh rosemary
   (plus more for garnish)
1 cup low-sodium chicken stock
½ tsp kosher salt
½ tsp freshly ground black pepper
1 tsp paprika
3 tsp chopped chives

How to make it
Preheat oven to 400° F.

Peel the potatoes, cutting the ends off flat so that each potato when sliced in half will stand up on its own. Then cut each potato in half crosswise.

Heat vegetable oil in a large cast iron pan or another heavy-duty, oven-proof skillet over medium-high heat. Sear the potatoes on top and bottom until golden brown, about 5 to 7 minutes each side.

Once the potatoes are browned, add the butter, garlic and the sprigs of thyme and rosemary. Stir and cook until the butter is melted and starts to brown, about 2 to 3 minutes.

Remove the pan from the heat and add the chicken stock and gently stir. Sprinkle the potatoes with kosher salt and freshly ground black pepper.

Place in a preheated oven and bake until the potatoes are tender, about 30 to 35 minutes.

Garnish with more rosemary sprigs, drizzle the potatoes with the pan juices and sprinkle chives on top.

Mashed Purple Sweet Potatoes with Coconut Milk, Lime and Ginger

Mashed purple sweet potatoes make a colorful and delicious side dish. They have become more popular in recent years and are available at many national grocery stores. Purple sweet potatoes are high in vitamin C and packed full of fiber.

Servings: 6

Ingredients
2 lbs purple sweet potatoes, peeled and cut into ½ inch slices
1 to 1½ cups canned coconut milk, unsweetened
1 lime, juiced
1½ tsp fresh grated ginger or ginger powder
½ tsp salt
1 tsp white pepper
4 tbsp unsalted butter
2 tbsp parsley, chopped (optional)

How to make it
Purple sweet potatoes take longer than regular potatoes to cook. Cutting them into ½ inch slices will help them cook faster. Bring a large pot of water to a simmer and add the potatoes. Cook for about 15 to 25 minutes, until fork tender.

Drain and return the potatoes to the pot. Add lime juice, ginger, butter, salt and white pepper. Pour in 1 cup of the coconut milk and mash the potatoes using a masher.

If you have one, use a stand or hand mixer to mash them. Mix until the ingredients are fully combined and the potatoes are fairly smooth, but still have a few lumps for texture. If the potatoes seem too dense, add more coconut milk.

Transfer to a serving bowl, top with additional butter and chopped parsley, if desired.

German Spätzle/Spaetzle (Tiny Egg Noodle Dumplings)

I love German spaetzle, but could never find it prepackaged in any local grocery store, so I would order it online. That was before I realized just how fast and easy it is to make. With just a few ingredients, these mini-dumplings can be made in 10 minutes. They are the perfect side dish for sauerbraten, but can go practically with anything. You can dress them up, by adding bacan, caramelized onions, cheese, sauteed mushrooms or whatever else you like.

Servings: 6

Ingredients
6 large eggs
1 cup whole milk
3½ cups all-purpose flour
1 tsp salt
½ tsp ground nutmeg (optional)
¼ tsp ground white pepper
¼ cup unsalted butter, melted
¼ cup fresh parsley, chopped

How to make it
In a medium bowl, whisk together the eggs and milk.

Add the flour, salt, nutmeg and white pepper to the bowl. Mix the ingredients until the batter is bubbly and elastic. The consistency of the batter should be pourable, but not runny.

Let the batter rest for 20 to 30 minutes at room temperature.

Bring a large pot of salted water to a boil.

Place spaetzle maker, grater or a colander over boiling water (I used a grader). Using a wooden spoon, press the dough through the holes and boil for 1 to 2 minutes or until spaetzle starts to float.

Remove with slotted spoon and place in a serving bowl or dish and toss with melted butter and fresh parsley. Serve immediately.

Portobello Stuffed Cabbage

Servings: 12 cabbage rolls

Ingredients

CABBAGE
1 large savoy cabbage

FILLING
3 cups portobello mushrooms, chopped
2 cups cooked rice (wild or white)
1 cup grated parmesan cheese
½ cup walnuts, chopped
1 yellow onion, chopped
½ bunch parsley, chopped
1 red bell pepper, seeded and chopped
2 egg whites
4 cloves garlic, chopped or minced
1 tsp crushed red pepper
1 tbsp extra-virgin olive oil
1 tbsp paprika
2 tbsp brown sugar
1 tbsp rosemary, chopped
1 tbsp sage
2 tbsp soy sauce
Juice of 1 lemon
Dash of salt and pepper

TOMATO SAUCE
2 (15-oz) cans crushed tomatoes
2 tbsp white wine vinegar
1 tbsp extra-virgin olive oil
2 cloves garlic, chopped or minced
1 tbsp brown sugar
Dash of pepper

How to make it

Remove core from cabbage, wash and throw the outer leaves away and seperate all its leaves. Fill a large pot with water, add 1 tbsp salt and bring to a boil. Carefully place the cabbage leaves into boiling water. Bring to a low boil and cook for 5 minutes. Remove the leaves from the water and let it cool while you mix the filling.

Combine filling ingredients in a large mixing bowl, mix well.

Before filling and rolling the cabbage, remove any hard outer veins from the leaves; this will make it easier to roll. Place about ½ cup of filling mixture near the stem end of a leaf. Roll the stem side over the filling, fold in the sides and roll up (see photos). Place rolls in a large casserole or baking dish.

In a separate large bowl, combine tomato sauce ingredients.

Preheat oven to 350° F.

Pour the tomato sauce over the cabbage rolls. Cover with foil and bake at 350° F for 1 hour. Uncover and continue baking for 30 minutes more, baste from time to time.

Buttery, Crispy, Parmesan-Herbed Potato Stacks

Baked potato stacks are a nice and delectable change from traditional potato dishes. This recipe makes a prefect side dish for the holiday season or anytime. They are flavored with herbs and parmesan cheese and have crispy edges and a buttery, creamy center. As they bake, they create a heavenly aroma in your kitchen.

Servings: 6

Ingredients
6 or 7 baby gold potatoes
¼ cup butter, melted
½ cup parmesan cheese, grated
1 tbsp olive oil
1 tsp fresh thyme, chopped
1 tsp fresh rosemary, chopped
2 garlic cloves, minced
1½ tsp coarse sea salt
½ tsp freshly ground black pepper
2 tbsp fresh chives, chopped

How to make it
Preheat oven to 400° F.

Spray 12-cup muffin pan with cooking spray and set aside.

Using a mandoline or sharp knife, cut the potatoes into 1/16-inch-thick slices.

Place the potato slices into a large bowl. Add melted butter, parmesan cheese, olive oil, thyme, rosemary, garlic, salt and pepper. Toss until evenly coated. (To ensure all the potatoes are evenly coated, I use my clean hands to toss.)

Layer the potato slices into stacks in the muffin cups. Fill each cup to the top.

Cover with foil and place on a baking sheet. Place in the oven and bake for 30 minutes. Remove the foil and continue baking until edges and tops are golden brown and centers are tender (20-30 minutes).

Remove from oven and let potato stacks cool in the pan for 5 minutes.

Carefully remove potato stacks from pan and transfer to a platter or individual plates. Drizzle any remaining butter in the muffin pan over the stacks and garnish with chives.

Incredible Bacon-Wrapped Mac and Cheese

By trial and error, I have mastered a way to successfully bake bacon-wrapped mac and cheese. The key is to use a small (7 x 10-inch), shallow baking dish. The small-size dish keeps the ingredients tight and compacted while baking. This helps to keep the serving from falling apart when plated.

Servings: 4

Ingredients
1 lb elbow macaroni
½ cup unsalted butter
¼ cup all-purpose flour
1 cup milk
¼ cup bread crumbs
3 cups sharp cheddar cheese, shredded
1 16-oz package thick-cut bacon
Salt and pepper to taste

How to make it
Preheat oven to 350° F.

Cook the pasta according to the instructions on the box, then drain and set aside.

In a large Dutch oven or large saucepan, melt the butter over medium heat. Add the flour and cook for 1 minute or until flour is golden and well-combined.

Reduce the heat to medium-low and slowly whisk in the milk until smooth. Simmer until slightly thickened (about 5 to 7 minutes), whisking occasionally.

Add the cheese, a cup at a time, whisking well after each addition and not adding more until the previous cup has fully melted; add the bread crumbs and stir until well combined. Season to taste with salt and pepper.

Add the drained pasta and stir to combine. Remove from heat and set aside.

See the photos below for this next part. In the baking dish, arrange the bacon strips in 8 rows with 2 strips of bacon in each row. The bacon should overlap the dish. Spread the mac and cheese evenly over the bacon. Fold the overlapping bacon strips over the mac and cheese and sprinkle a little pepper on top.

Bake 15-20 minutes, then put under the broiler for a few minutes until the top of the bacon is brown and crisp. Don't let it char.

Let cool for 10 minutes, then slice into 4 servings and place them on a paper towel-lined plate. Allow the paper towels to absorb the extra bacon grease before serving.

Classic German Red Cabbage (Rotkohl)

This sweet and sour cabbage is an easy side dish to make. It's traditionally served with German sauerbraten and spaetzle (see pages 112 and 82). It also goes well with other beef dishes, chicken, pork or almost anything else.

Red cabbage is one of the healthiest foods you can eat. It's a good source of vitamins and provides small amounts of calcium, magnesium and zinc, which can help build and maintain healthy bones.

If properly stored, a fresh head of red cabbage can last from 3 weeks to up to 2 months in your refrigerator.

Servings: 4

Ingredients
2 tbsp butter
1 Granny Smith or other semi-tart apple, peeled, cored and diced
1 small yellow onion, chopped
4 cups shredded red cabbage (about half a head)
¼ cup white vinegar
4 tbsp sugar
½ cup red wine
1 tsp ground cloves
1 tsp ground allspice

How to make it
In a large skillet or Dutch oven, melt butter over medium-high heat. Once melted, add the onions and apples. Reduce heat to medium-low and sauté until soft (about 6-7 minutes).

Add shredded cabbage, apple cider vinegar, sugar and red wine. Cover with lid and cook until cabbage is tender (about 12-15 minutes).

Add the ground clove and allspice, and stir until well combined. Cover and simmer over medium-low heat for 30-35 minutes stirring occasionally until the cabbage is tender.

Remove lid and simmer uncovered until the sauce has thickened (about 10-15 minutes).

Check the taste; add sugar, ground cloves, salt and black pepper if needed.

A Piece of Time

Burgers

Smoked Sirloin, Brie, Bacon Burgers with Merlot-Portabellos

Servings: 6

Ingredients

PATTIES
2 lbs ground sirloin
3 cloves garlic, minced
Salt and pepper to taste

TOPPINGS
2.5-oz package
   fully cooked bacon
7 oz brie cheese wedge
   (cut into ¼ inch-thick slices)
6 large portabello tops
½ cup Merlot wine
Spicy mustard to taste

BUNS
6 whole-wheat buns

How to make it

Mix ingredients for patties in a medium-size bowl. I find it best to use your hands for mixing. Form mixture into six even patties. Place patties on a sheet of wax paper until ready for smoking.

Place portabello tops, stem side up, into a shallow bowl or dish. Pour a ½ cup of Merlot wine over the portabellos and sprinkle with a dash of salt and pepper. Set aside until ready for grilling.

Note: Techniques for using wood chips vary by manufacturer and style of grill or smoker you use. Please refer to your owner's manual for proper usage.

Pre-heat grill/smoker to 275° F, add wood chips. Place sirloin patties on rack and smoke at 275° F for 45-60 minutes depending on how well done you want them. Place slices of bacon and brie cheese on top of each burger. Let melt for about one minute. Remove from grill and set aside.

Place the wine-soaked portabellos on rack with stem sides up and smoke for about 10 minutes, flip and cook for another 10 minutes. Remove and place on paper towel until you are ready for topping the burgers.

Place burgers with bacon and brie on bottom half of whole-wheat buns; top burgers with portabellos and a little spicy mustard. Cover with top of bun and serve.

Caribbean Burgers with Tropical Fruit Salsa

Servings: 6

Ingredients

SALSA
1 cup fresh pineapple, finely chopped
1 ripe mango, peeled, seeded and finely chopped
1 tsp cinnamon
¼ cup red bell pepper, seeded and finely chopped
¼ cup red onion, finely chopped
¼ cup cilantro, finely chopped
1 tsp brown sugar
1 jalapeño, seeded and minced

PATTIES
2½ lbs ground beef
3 cloves garlic, minced
1 small onion, finely diced
1 tsp ground allspice
1 tsp crushed red pepper flakes
1 tsp ground nutmeg
1 tsp cayenne pepper
1 tsp cinnamon
2 tsp brown sugar
¼ tsp salt

TOPPINGS
6 tomato slices
6 crisp iceberg lettuce leaves

BUNS
6 burger buns, split and lightly toasted on the grill

How to make it

SALSA
Combine all of the salsa ingredients in a medium-size bowl; mix well and refrigerate until ready to use. The salsa will keep for 2 to 3 days in the fridge.

PATTIES
Mix ingredients for patties in a medium-size bowl. Form mixture into six even patties. Place patties on a sheet of wax paper until ready for grilling.

Preheat grill for high heat, place beef patties on grill for about 5 minutes on each side.

Remove from grill and place patties on bottom half of buns, place pineapple slices on cooked patties (one per burger), add grilled red bell peppers (two per burger) and remaining toppings.

Cover each burger with the top of a bun and serve.

Gyro-Inspired Greek Lamb Burgers with Tzatziki Yogurt

I love experimenting in my kitchen and coming up with new twists to some of my favorite foods. I often ask my family and friends to rate my creations. This one was a big hit.

Servings: 6

Ingredients
TZATZIKI YOGURT
3 tsp olive oil
1 tsp white vinegar
2 cloves garlic (finely minced)
½ tsp salt
½ tsp white pepper
1 cup Greek yogurt
1 cup sour cream
1 large, seedless cucumber (peeled and finely diced)
1 tsp chopped fresh dill

PATTIES
2 lbs ground lamb
6 garlic cloves, minced
1 tsp ground oregano
1 cup crumbled feta cheese
1 tsp freshly ground black pepper
½ tsp salt

TOPPINGS
18 cucumber slices
6 tomato slices
24 mild banana pepper rings
2.25-oz can black olive slices, drained
1 medium white onion, sliced
6 crisp iceberg lettuce leaves

BUNS
6 sesame seed buns, split and lightly toasted on the grill

How to make it
TZATZIKI YOGURT
Combine all of the tzatziki yogurt ingredients in a medium-size bowl; mix well and refrigerate for at least 2 hours before serving.

PATTIES
Mix ingredients for patties in a medium-size bowl. Form mixture into six even patties. Place patties on a sheet of wax paper until ready for grilling. Preheat grill for high heat; place beef patties on grill for about 5 to 7 minutes on each side.

Remove from grill and place patties on bottom half of buns, place 3 cucumber slices on each burger, add remaining toppings (in order as listed above) and spread tzatziki yogurt on buns and serve.

Hot Buffalo, Bacon, Blue Burgers with Celery Salsa

This is an awesome burger! But like Buffalo wings, a little messy ... but then again, only the best burgers are. Have your napkins ready and enjoy!

Servings: 6

Ingredients
CELERY SALSA
1 cup celery, diced
½ cup onion, finely chopped
1 jalapeño pepper, seeded and finely diced
2 clove garlic, minced
1 medium tomato, diced
¼ cup hot pepper or Buffalo wing sauce
3 tsp brown sugar
2 tsp white vinegar
¼ tsp paprika
¼ tsp white pepper

BURGERS
2 lbs ground beef
4 cloves garlic, minced
8 to 10 slices bacon, cooked crisp and crumbled
1 cup crumbled blue cheese
2 eggs, beaten
1 tsp crushed red pepper flakes
1 tsp freshly ground black pepper
¼ tsp salt

TOPPINGS (optional)
6 crisp iceberg lettuce leaves
6 tomato slices
Bread and butter pickle slices
Chunky blue cheese dressing

BUNS
6 onion buns, split and lightly toasted on the grill

How to make it
CELERY SALSA
Mix ingredients for the slalsa in a medium-size bowl. Place in refrigerator and let chill for at least one hour before using.

PATTIES
Mix ingredients for patties in a medium bowl. I find it best to use your hands for mixing. Form mixture into six even patties. Place patties on a sheet of wax paper until ready for grilling. Preheat grill for high heat, place beef patties on grill for about 5 minutes on each side.

Remove from grill and place patties on bottom half of onion buns, add the topping, and celery salsa, cover with top of bun and serve.

Thanksgiving Turkey Burgers with Stuffing and Cranberry Sauce

Enjoy your favorite holiday flavors anytime of the year with these juicy and delicious turkey burgers. I like to serve them with steak fries and a side of turkey gravy.

Servings: 6

Ingredients
PATTIES
2 lb ground turkey
2 eggs
6-oz box of seasoned, stuffing mix (I use the Stove Top brand)
½ cup yellow onion, finely chopped
2 tsp fresh rosemary, chopped
½ tsp salt
½ tsp black pepper
6 slices provolone or Swiss cheese
14-oz can whole-berry cranberry sauce
6 hamburger buns
3 to 4 tsp olive oil

OPTIONAL TOPPINGS
Romaine or iceburg lettuce
Tomato slices
Pickle slices
Onion slices
Mayonnaise

How to make it
In a large mixing bowl, mix together the ground turkey, eggs, stuffing mix, onion, rosemary, salt and pepper.

Mix until well combined and let stand for 20 minutes to allow the stuffing mix to absorb moisture from the eggs and turkey.

Divide the mixture into 6 equal portions and shape into burger patties.

Preheat olive oil in a 12-inch non-stick or cast iron skillet over medium-high heat.

Add 4 of the turkey patties and sear until golden brown on bottom, about 4 or 5 minutes, flip and continue to cook until cooked through, about 4 or 5 minutes longer. The center should register 165° F on an instant-read thermometer.

With the burgers still in the pan, top with a slice of provolone or Swiss cheese. Heat until cheese is melted, covering the pan if needed. Remove cooked patties and place on a dish.

Repeat cooking method with remaining turkey patties.

Place burgers on buns and top with a tablespoon or two of cranberry sauce.

Free Your Humanity

Meat

Flank Steak with Avocado Chimichurri Sauce

My mouth waters just thinking about this recipe. This juicy and delicious steak and homemade avocado chimichurri is easy to make and is ready in less than 30 minutes.

Chimichurri sauce is traditionally served with grilled meats, but it's also awesome served with chicken or used as a dip with vegetables and bread or chips.

Servings: 6

Ingredients
AVOCADO CHIMICHURRI SAUCE
1 cup fresh cilantro, chopped
¼ cup fresh parsley, chopped
1 tbsp fresh oregano, chopped
3 cloves garlic minced
¼ cup apple cider vinegar
4 tbsp olive oil
Juice of 2 limes
Zest and juice of 1 lemon
½ tsp red pepper flakes
1 tsp white pepper
3 avocados, peeled, pitted and diced

2 lb flank steak
1 tbsp ground cumin
1½ tsp salt
1 tsp fresh ground pepper
2 tbsp olive oil

How to make it
AVOCADO CHIMICHURRI SAUCE
Add the cilantro, parsley, oregano, garlic, vinegar, olive oil, lime juice, lemon zest and juice, red pepper flakes and white pepper to a food processor; pulse until herbs are finely chopped.

Transfer the sauce mixture to a mixing bowl and add the diced avocado and gently stir to combine. Cover and refrigerate until ready to use.

If the flank steak is too long to fix in your pan, cut it across the grain into 2 smaller pieces.

In a small bowl, mix together the cumin, salt and pepper. Pat steak dry on both sides with paper towels and rub the mixture on both sides of the steak.

Heat a grill pan or large skillet over high heat; once hot, add the olive oil.

Sear the steak over high heat, until browned (about 2 to 4 minutes on each side). Transfer to a cutting board, loosely cover with foil and let rest for 5 to 10 minutes.

Carve the steak against the grain, in ¼ inch-thick slices and transfer to a platter. Spoon the chimichurri sauce on the top and serve.

Palomilla Steak

Servings: 4

Ingredients
4, 8 oz top sirloin steaks,
    pounded to ¼-inch thickness
½ tsp ground coriander
½ tsp ground cumin
1 tsp black pepper
1 garlic powder
1 tsp salt
1 large-size white onion, finely chopped
Juice of 3 limes (divided)
½ cup fresh cilantro, chopped
¼ cup fresh parsley, chopped
2 tbsp olive oil
2 tbsp butter (divided)
1 garlic clove, minced

How to make it
In a small bowl, mix together the coriander, cumin, black pepper, garlic powder and salt.

Generously season the steak on both sides, massaging the spice mixture into the beef. Cover and refrigerate for at least 1 hour.

Meanwhile, combine the chopped onion, ⅔ lime juice, cilanto and parsley in a bowl and set aside.

Heat the olive oil and 1 tbsp of the butter in a skillet over medium-high heat. Remove the steaks from the marinade and pat dry. Cook the steaks, one at a time, for 2 to 3 minutes on each side.

Turn the heat down to medium low. Add the remaining lime juice, minced garlic and the remaining tbsp of butter. Deglaze the pan and pour the juices, butter and garlic mixture evenly over the four steaks.

Garnish the steaks with the onion and parsley mixture and serve immediately.

This is great served with black beans, white rice and sautéed or fried sweet plantains.

Stir-Fried Beef and Vegetables

Ingredients

STIR FRY
1½ lbs thinly sliced steak such as flank or sirloin
1 cup broccoli florets
1 15-oz can whole baby corn, drained
1 red bell pepper, seeded and sliced into strips
1 green bell pepper, seeded and sliced into strips
1 onion, chopped
Salt and pepper to taste
2 tbsp vegetable oil

SAUCE
¼ cup soy sauce
½ cup water
¼ cup brown sugar
1 tsp minced garlic
1 tsp minced ginger
⅓ cup hoisin sauce
2 tsp corn starch

How to make it

SAUCE
Place the soy sauce, water, brown sugar, garlic, ginger and hoisin sauce in a small pot over medium-high heat. Stir for about 3 minutes until sugar is dissolved. Turn up heat to high and bring to a boil.

Mix the cornstarch with 2 to 3 tsp of water until dissolved. Add the cornstarch mixture to the sauce and boil for 1-2 minutes or until sauce has thickened. Set sauce aside.

STIR FRY
Heat 1 tbsp of vegetable oil in a large pan over medium-high heat. Add the vegetables and season with salt and pepper to taste.

Cook for 3-4 minutes or until vegetables have started to brown and soften. Remove them from the pan and set aside.

Wipe out the pan. Heat the remaining 1 tbsp of oil in the pan over medium-high heat.

Place half of the steak in the pan and season with salt and pepper. Cook for 2-3 minutes on each side or until just cooked through.

Set the first batch of steak aside and repeat the process with the remaining beef.

Add all of the meat and vegetables back to the pan. Pour the sauce over the top and cook for 2-3 minutes over medium-high heat until warmed through.

German Sauerbraten

Servings: 6 to 8

Ingredients
MARINADE
1 cup red wine vinegar
½ bottle red wine
10 whole black peppercorns, cracked
1 tsp salt
1 bay leaf
6 whole cloves
2 cloves garlic, chopped
2 tsp lemon rind
1 medium onion, chopped
1 tsp nutmeg
3 celery stalks, finely chopped
2 large carrots, finely chopped
3 parsley sprigs

ROAST
5 to 6 lbs beef chuck roast or rump roast
3 tbsp olive oil
8 gingersnap cookies, crushed
Salt and pepper to taste

How to make it
In a large non-reactive pot such as cast iron (I use a Dutch oven), combine all of the marinade ingredients and bring to a boil over medium-high heat. Reduce heat to low and simmer for five minutes. Remove from heat and allow the marinade to cool.

Submerge the roast in the marinade and refrigerate for at least 3 days and up to 2 weeks. Turn the roast daily while marinating.

Remove the roast from the marinade, pat dry with paper towels and set it aside. Transfer the marinade to a bowl.

Wipe out the inside of the pot with paper towels. Lightly coat the bottom of the pot with oil and heat until quite hot, but not smoking. Sear the roast on all sides until browned (about 2 to 3 minutes per side). Reduce heat to medium-high and return the marinade to the pot with the meat.

Choose how you would like to cook the sauerbraten: either turn the heat down, cover, and let gently simmer on the stove for 2 to 2½ hours, until the meat is tender, or cover and place the pot into a 350° F oven for the same amount of time. Whichever method you use, you will want the pot to be a gentle simmer, not a rolling boil, so adjust heat accordingly and check it a few times during the cooking process.

Remove meat from the cooking liquids, place on a cutting board and let it rest for 10 to 15 minutes.

Meanwhile, strain the contents of the pot and discard the solids. Return the liquid to the pot.

Add the crushed gingersnaps to the marinade. Cook and stir over medium-low heat for 10 minutes until thickened to a gravy. If needed, add salt and pepper to taste.

Slice the sauerbraten and serve, topped with hot gravy. Serve extra gravy on the side.

Asian-Style Pepper Steak

Servings: 4

Ingredients
1½ lb flank or sirloin steak, cut into
    ¼ inch-thick strips
2 tbsp soy sauce
2 tbsp red wine
4 tbsp olive oil
1 large onion, julienned
1 red bell pepper, seeded and julienned
1 green bell pepper, seeded and julienned

SAUCE
¼ cup soy sauce
2 tbsp cornstarch
⅓ cup red wine
⅓ cup low-sodium chicken broth
1 tbsp olive oil
2 tbsp brown sugar
2 cloves garlic, minced
2 tbsp ginger, fresh, minced or grated
2 tsp black pepper
½ tsp salt

How to make it
In a medium-size bowl, whisk all of the sauce ingredients and set aside.

Add the steak strips, soy sauce and red wine to a bowl, toss together and let it sit for 10 or 15 minutes to marinate.

In a large skillet or wok, heat olive oil over high heat. Once the oil is hot, add the steak strips and marinade, cook for 4-5 minutes, or until lightly browned, stirring occasionally.

Add the onion and peppers and everything else together; cook for 2 to 3 minutes until the vegetables start to soften a bit.

Pour the sauce over the beef and veggies, and cook for another minute or until the sauce thickens.

Serve over cooked rice or rice noodles.

Mshikaki Steak Kebabs with Tomato Onion Sauce

Mshikaki is a popular dish made and sold by street vendors in Tanzania and Kenya. The name refers to skewered pieces of marinated meat that is slowly cooked over hot coals. It's served with sauces or dips on the side.

Servings: 6

Ingredients

SPICE BLEND
2 tsp curry powder
1½ tsp garlic powder
1 tsp sea salt
1 tsp ground cayenne pepper
1 tsp ground ginger
1 tsp ground cloves

STEAK KEBABS
1 cup crushed tomatoes
¼ cup chopped fresh papaya
3 tbsp lemon juice
2 tbsp olive oil
2 lbs sirloin beef, cut into 1-inch cubes

TOMATO ONION SAUCE
1 tbsp olive oil
1 cup yellow onion, chopped
2 cups crushed tomatoes
¼ cup water
3 tbsp lemon juice
2 tbsp tomato paste
2 tbsp honey
½ tsp sea salt

GARNISH
½ cup cilantro, chopped

How to make it

SPICE BLEND
In a small bowl, mix all of the spice blend ingredients until well blended. Save 1 tsp for the tomato onion sauce.

STEAK KEBABS
Place the tomatoes, papaya, lemon juice, olive oil and spice blend into a blender or food processor. Purée until smooth. Pour mixture into a large sealable plastic bag or an airtight container. Add beef cubes and toss to coat well. Place in a refrigerator for 2 hours or overnight.

TOMATO ONION SAUCE
Place all of the sauce ingredients along with the remaining spice blend into blender or food processor and purée until smooth.

Pour the mixture into a sauce pan, stir and bring to boil. Reduce heat to low and simmer for 10 minutes, stirring occasionally.

Remove the beef from the marinade. Do not discard any remaining marinade. Thread beef onto skewers. Brush on the remaining marinade and grill over medium-high heat 5 to 6 minutes per side or until done to your liking.

Garnish with cilantro and serve with the Tomato Onion Sauce on the side.

Philly Steak Mac and Cheese

Servings: 4

Ingredients
4 tbsp olive oil, divided
1½ to 2 lbs tenderloin or sirloin steak, thinly sliced against the grain
2 yellow onions, thinly sliced
2 green bell peppers, seeded and thinly sliced
1 tsp ground mustard
1 tsp ground cayenne pepper
1 tsp kosher salt
1½ tsp freshly ground black pepper
¼ cup all-purpose flour
2 tbsp Worcestershire sauce
1 lb elbow macaroni
¼ cup unsalted butter, melted
1 cup beef broth
2 cups heavy cream
2 cups shredded provolone
2 cups shredded white cheddar cheese

How to make it
Preheat oven to 350° F. Spray a 13 x 9-inch baking dish with cooking spray.

Place the steak slices in a medium-size bowl and season with ground mustard, cayenne pepper, salt and black pepper. Mix well and set aside.

Heat 2 tbsp of olive oil in a large nonstick skillet over medium-high heat and sauté the onion and green peppers until the peppers are lightly browned and onions turn translucent. Remove from pan and set aside.

Using the same skillet, heat 2 tbsp of olive oil and place the steak in a single layer; you may have to work in batches, depending on the size of your pan. Crowding the pan prevents the steak from browning nicely. Cook for about 2-3 minutes on each side. Repeat with remaining steak slices if needed. Remove the pan from heat, whisk in flour and top with Worcestershire sauce.

In a large pot, prepare macaroni according to package directions. Drain and return to the pot. Add the steak, onions and green peppers along with the remaining ingredients and mix well.

Pour the macaroni mixture into the baking dish. Bake 25 to 30 minutes or until mixture is hot (at least 165° F in center) and the cheese is melted.

Rich and Creamy Beef Stroganoff

Beef Stroganoff originated in Russia in the mid-19th century. Today it's a popular dish around the world, with countless variations of the original recipe. Serve this tasty recipe over cooked egg noodles, pasta, rice or mashed potatoes.

Servings: 4

Ingredients
2 lbs boneless ribeye or sirloin beef
4 tbsp grapeseed or vegetable oil
3 tbsp unsalted butter, softened
1 yellow onion, sliced
2 garlic cloves, minced
8 oz baby bella mushrooms, sliced
2 tbsp all-purpose flour
2 cups beef broth
2 tbsp Worcestershire sauce
1 tbsp Dijon mustard
½ tsp crushed red pepper flakes
1 cup sour cream
Salt and pepper to taste
2 tbsp parsley, chopped (optional)

How to make it
Trim off and discard any excess fat from the beef. Use meat mallet or rolling pin to flatten the steaks to about ⅓-inch thickness. Slice into ½-inch strips.

Heat 2 tbsp of oil in a large skillet over high heat. Place half the beef in the skillet; cook and stir until browned (about 5 to 7 minutes), then transfer to a plate.

Add the remaining 2 tbsp oil and repeat with remaining beef. Transfer beef to a plate and set aside.

Reduce heat to medium high. Add butter, melt. Stir in the onion and garlic. Cook and stir until the onion is soft and translucent, then add the mushrooms. Cook until the mushrooms are tender and golden (about 10 minutes).

Sprinkle the flour over the onions and mushrooms, cook, stirring, for 1 minute. Slowly add half the broth while stirring. Once incorporated, add the remaining broth.

Add the Worcestershire sauce, mustard and red pepper. Stir until incorporated.

Return the beef to skillet. Bring to a simmer, cover and cook on low for about 1 hour. Stir often.

Slowly stir in the sour cream and season with more salt and pepper, if needed.

Serve over egg noodles, pasta, rice or mashed potatoes.

Sprinkle with chopped parsley if desired.

Irish Shepherd's Pie with Beef Tenderloin Tips

Servings: 6

Ingredients

FILLING
2 tbsp olive oil
2 lb beef tenderloin tips, cut into 1-inch pieces
1 medium yellow onion, diced
3 garlic cloves, minced
2 tbsp all purpose flour
1 (6-oz can) tomato paste
1 cup frozen carrots
1 cup frozen peas
1 cup frozen corn kernels
1 tbsp dried parsley
1 tsp dried rosemary
1 tsp dried thyme
1 cup beef broth
2 tsp Worcestershire sauce
1 tsp salt
½ tsp ground black pepper

POTATO TOPPING
2 lb russet potatoes, peeled and cut into wedges
¼ cup unsalted butter, melted
¾ cup of heavy cream
½ tsp salt
¼ tsp ground black pepper

How to make it

FILLING
Heat olive oil in a Dutch oven or cast iron skillet over medium-high heat until shimmering. Add the beef tips in a single layer without crowding. You may need to work in batches. Brown the tips on all sides. Transfer the tips to a plate and set aside.

Save the beef drippings in the skillet and reduce the heat to medium. Add the onions and cook for 4 minutes, stirring occasionally. Add garlic and cook for 1 minute. Add flour and tomato paste, stir until well combined.

Increase the heat to medium-high, add the remaining ingredients. Stir occasionally until it reaches a low boil, reduce heat and simmer for 20-25 minutes until the liquid has been reduced. Return the beef tips to the pan. Turn off the heat and set aside.

Preheat oven to 350° F.

POTATO TOPPING
Place the potatoes in a large pot, add cold water until the potatoes are covered. Bring the water to a boil. Reduce to a simmer and cook until the potatoes are fork tender (about 15 to 25 minutes).

Drain the potatoes and return them back to the pot. Mash the potatoes with butter. Add the heavy cream, salt and pepper, and stir until well mixed.

Pour the meat mixture into a 2-quart baking dish. Spread it out into an even layer. Spoon the mashed potatoes on top of the meat. Carefully spread into an even layer. If you want to get fancy, you could pipe mashed potatoes over the meat mixture, as shown in the photo.

Bake uncovered for 25-30 minutes.

Cool for 10 or 15 minutes before serving.

Lime Chicken with Blueberry Bourbon Sauce

Servings: 4

Ingredients

LIME CHICKEN
Zest of 1 lime
½ cup fresh lime juice
¼ cup olive oil
¼ cup honey
1 tsp salt
1 tsp freshly ground black pepper
4 boneless, skinless, chicken breasts

BLUEBERRY BOURBON SAUCE
2¼ cup blueberries, divided
1 onion, chopped
1 jalapeño, seeded and chopped
1 cup ketchup
½ cup brown sugar
½ tsp allspice
½ apple cider vinegar
½ cup bourbon
1 tsp hot pepper sauce

GARNISH
Lime wedges
¼ cup blueberries

How to make it

LIME CHICKEN
Place the lime zest and juice, olive oil, honey, salt and pepper into a resealable container or a large freezer bag. Mix well and add the chicken breasts. Make sure all of the breasts are covered with the marinade. Seal the container and place in the refrigerator for at least two hours or overnight to marinate.

Heat 2 tsp olive oil in a grill pan or large heavy skillet over high heat. Add the chicken breasts and cook for 5 to 6 minutes on each side or until cooked through. (The internal temp should be 165 degrees.) Remove the chicken from the pan and let rest for 5 minutes before serving.

BLUEBERRY BOURBON SAUCE
Place 2 cups of blueberries and the remaining sauce ingredients into a blender or food processor and purée smooth.

Transfer the liquid to a saucepan and bring to a boil over medium heat. Reduce heat to low and simmer for 15 to 20 minutes, stirring occasionally. Remove from heat.

Serve the chicken with the blueberry sauce drizzled on a plate and garnish with lime wedges and the remaining blueberries.

Papaya Chicken Curry with Coconut Rice

Servings: 4

Ingredients

PAPAYA CHICKEN CURRY
2 tbsp olive oil
4 tbsp red curry paste
2 cloves of garlic
1 large papaya, peeled, seeded and cut into 2" to 3" cubes
14-oz can coconut milk
2 boneless, skinless chicken breasts, cut into 1" to 2" cubes
1 red bell pepper, seeded and julienned
2 tbsp finely minced, fresh parsley

COCONUT RICE
2 cups jasmine rice
14-oz can coconut milk
1½ to 2 cups water
1 tsp kosher salt

How to make it

In a large pot over medium heat, combine rice, coconut milk, 1½ cups of water and salt. Bring to a boil, then reduce heat and let simmer, covered, 18 to 20 minutes or until rice is tender. If needed, add the remaining ½ cup of water.

While the rice is cooking, place the curry paste, garlic, papaya and the coconut milk in a blender. Blend until the ingredients are well combined and smooth.

Heat the olive oil in a large pot to medium heat, add the chicken and cook until lightly brown, then pour in the mixture from the blender and add the red bell pepper slices. Let everything simmer for about 10 minutes.

Once the rice has cooked, remove it from the heat and let sit for 10 minutes, then fluff with a fork.

Serve the papaya chicken curry over the rice and garnish with parsley.

Chicken Piccata

Chicken Piccata is one of my all-time favorite recipes. I was a little intimidated the first time I made it, because I thought it would be difficult; but to my surprise, it's very easy to make. I like to serve this over pasta, topped with the remaining sauce from the pan. Roasted asparagus or green beans makes for a delicious side.

Servings: 4

Ingredients
2 large boneless, skinless, chicken breasts
1 tsp salt
1 tsp black pepper
½ cup all-purpose flour
6 tbsp extra-virgin olive oil, divided
6 tbsp unsalted butter, divided
1 cup chicken stock
¼ cup lemon juice
1 clove minced garlic
4 tbsp capers, drained
1 tbsp corn starch slurry
4 tbsp fresh parsley, chopped (optional)

How to make it
Butterfly each chicken breast and cut in half lengthwise so you have 4 pieces of chicken.

Lay a piece of plastic wrap or parchment paper on top and pound to about ¼-inch thick. Season both sides with salt and pepper.

Add the flour to a shallow bowl and dredge each piece of chicken in flour, shaking off the excess.

Heat 3 tbsp of olive oil and 3 tbsp of butter in a large skillet over medium-high heat. Fry the chicken until golden brown, about 3-4 minutes per side. Fry two at a time, so not to over-crowd the pan. Remove the chicken from the pan and set aside on a plate.

Drain the oil from the pan and wipe away and discard any remains of the fried flour with a paper towel. (This will avoid any chance of a burnt taste or look when finished.)

Reheat the pan to medium-heat, add 3 tbsp of olive oil and 3 tbsp of butter and carefully pour in the chicken stock and lemon juice. In a small bowl, make a slurry with the cornstarch and cold water, and slowly whisk into the simmering sauce. Add the garlic and capers, and cook until the sauce has slightly thickened; about 4-5 minutes. Reduce heat to low and return the chicken to the pan.

Coat the chicken with the sauce. Add lemon slices and simmer for 2 minutes, until the sauce thickens slightly, sprinkle with parsley (optional), then remove from the heat and serve.

Artichoke Chicken with Bow Tie Pasta

I ordered this at a restaurant in Naples, Florida, many years ago. I was overwhelmed with the flavor of this eye-catching dish. I was determined to recreate it with my own twist. To this day, it is one of my favorite pasta dishes.

Servings: 4

Ingredients
1 lb uncooked bow tie pasta
2 tsp corn starch
½ cup chicken broth
3 tsp olive oil, divided
1 onion, chopped
¼ tsp salt
¼ tsp black pepper to taste
1 lb boneless skinless chicken breasts, cut into bite-size chunks
½ cup sliced fresh mushrooms
2.25-oz can sliced black olives, drained
½ cup cherry tomatoes, halved
2 garlic cloves, minced
12-oz jar marinated, artichoke hearts, quartered or roman style; do not drain
1 tsp dried oregano
2 tbsp fresh parsley, minced
½ cup fresh grated, parmesan cheese

How to make it
Cook bow tie pasta according to package directions, drain and set aside.

Meanwhile, in a small bowl, mix corn starch and broth until smooth.

In a large skillet, heat 2 tsp olive oil over medium heat. Add onion, salt and pepper and cook 1-2 minutes until translucent; add chicken and cook 2-4 minutes longer or until its no longer pink. Remove from pan.

In the same skillet, heat remaining oil over medium-high heat. Add mushrooms, black olives, tomatoes and garlic, and cook 2 minutes. Gently stir in artichoke hearts, oregano and corn starch mixture. Bring to a boil and cook and stir until thickened, 2 to 3 minutes.

Add bow tie pasta, chicken and parsley and heat through, tossing to combine.

Sprinkle with parmesan cheese and serve.

Sesame-Ginger Chicken

Servings: 4

Ingredients
3 tbsp toasted sesame seeds
3 tsp fresh grated ginger
1 tsp minced garlic
½ cup honey
1½ tbsp soy sauce
2 tbsp light brown sugar
3 tbsp fresh orange juice
2 large boneless, skinless, chicken breasts
2 tsp olive oil
2 tbsp sliced green onions

How to make it
Combine the sesame seeds, ginger, garlic, honey, soy sauce, brown sugar and orange juice in a small bowl. Whisk until combined and set aside.

Butterfly each chicken breast and cut in half lengthwise so you have 4 pieces of chicken.

Lay a piece of plastic wrap or parchment paper on top and pound to about ½-inch thick.

Coat a large nonstick skillet pan with olive oil and heat over medium-high. Add the chicken and cook 4 to 5 minutes on each side until golden brown.

Reduce heat to low and slowly pour the sesame-ginger mixture over the chicken and cook for an additional 5 minutes.

Garnish with sliced green onions and serve.

Firecracker Chicken

Servings: 4

Ingredients
1½ lb boneless, skinless, chicken breasts, cut into 1-inch pieces
3 eggs, well beaten
¼ cup cornstarch
½ tsp salt
½ tsp black pepper
¼ cup grapeseed oil
½ cup buffalo hot sauce
½ cup brown sugar
1 clove garlic, minced
1 tbsp white vinegar
½ tsp red pepper flakes
1 tsp soy sauce
¼ cup sliced green onions
Cooking spray

How to make it
Preheat the oven to 350° F. Coat a 9"x13" or equivalent-size pan with cooking spray.

Place the chicken pieces and the well-beaten eggs in a medium-size bowl and lightly toss until evenly coated.

In a large, shallow bowl, whisk cornstarch, salt and black pepper.

Dip each piece of the egg-coated chicken into the cornstarch mixture.

Heat the grapeseed oil over medium-high heat in a large pan. Place the chicken in a single layer and cook until golden and crispy, about 3 to 4 minutes on each side. You may have to work in batches.

Transfer the cooked chicken to a paper towel-lined plate.

In a small bowl, whisk together the buffalo sauce, brown sugar, garlic, vinegar, red pepper flakes and soy sauce.

Place the chicken pieces in a single layer in the 9"x13" pan.

Pour the sauce over the chicken. Bake for 30 to 40 minutes, stirring once halfway through to coat the chicken with the sauce.

Serve with jasmine rice and top with green onions or sesame seeds.

Tequila-Lime Chicken Tacos with Creamy Cilantro-Jalapeño Sauce

Servings: 4 tacos

Ingredients
½ cup tequila
¼ cup fresh lime juice
2 cloves garlic, minced
2 jalapeños: 1 seeded and finely chopped and 1 sliced, divided
½ tsp black pepper
½ tsp salt
1 lb boneless, skinless chicken breasts
1 tbsp olive oil
4 corn tortillas, warmed, for serving
1 avocado, peeled, pitted and sliced
¼ head red cabbage, shredded
½ cup cherry tomatoes, halved
½ cup cotija cheese, shredded

Lime wedges and jalapeño slices for serving

SAUCE
2 jalapeños, halved and seeded
2 cups loosely packed cilantro, stems removed
½ cup sour cream
2 cloves garlic, minced
Juice of 1 lime
½ tsp salt
½ cup olive oil
1 tbsp white vinegar

How to make it
In a large baking dish, whisk together tequila, lime juice, garlic, chopped jalapeños and salt and pepper. Add chicken and marinate in the fridge for at least 30 minutes and up to 2 hours.

Heat olive oil in a grill pan or skillet over medium-high heat. Cook chicken until golden and no longer pink inside, about 6 to 8 minutes per side. Let rest 10 minutes before slicing. Cut the chicken into ¼-inch slices.

Serve in warm tortillas with avocado slices, cabbage, tomatoes, sliced jalapeño and cotija, and squeeze with lime.

SAUCE
Place the jalapeños, cilantro, sour cream, garlic, lime juice and salt in the blender or food processor. With the motor running, add olive oil and vinegar in a slow stream until the sauce is smooth and creamy.

The sauce can store in the refrigerator for up to one week.

Coconut Pineapple Chicken with Coconut Rice

Servings: 4

Ingredients

MARINADE
2 cups pineapple juice
¼ cup soy sauce
¼ cup apple cider vinegar
3 cloves garlic, minced
1 tsp grated ginger
½ tsp ground cloves or allspice
½ tsp white pepper

CHICKEN
2 lb boneless chicken breast, cut into bite-size cubes
2 cups flaked coconut
1 cup panko bread crumbs
1 cup fresh pineapple, cubed
1 orange or red bell pepper, seeded and chopped
1 small red onion, chopped
2 tsp fresh mint, chopped (optional)
2 tsp toasted sesame seeds (optional)

COCONUT RICE
2 cups jasmine rice
14-oz can coconut milk
1½ cups water

How to make it

MARINADE
Mix all of the marinade ingredients together in a bowl and set aside.

CHICKEN
Place the chicken in a large, sealable, plastic bag or an airtight container. Add the marinade and refrigerate for at least 1 hour.

Preheat oven to 400° F.

Line a large baking sheet with parchment paper and spray lightly with baking spray. Evenly spread the coconut and bread crumbs on the parchment paper. Place in oven for 5 minutes or until lightly toasted. Remove from oven, let cool and then place in a large bowl. You can use the same baking sheet and parchment paper to bake the chicken.

Remove chicken from refrigerator. Using tongs, coat each chicken piece with coconut and place on parchment paper. Arrange the pineapple, bell peppers and onions around the chicken. Bake for 15 to 20 minutes or until the chicken is no longer pink and the internal temperature is 165° F.

COCONUT RICE
In a large pot over medium heat, combine rice, coconut milk, water and salt. Bring to a boil, then reduce heat, cover and let simmer for 15 to 20 minutes or until rice is tender. Remove from heat and let sit for 10 minutes, then fluff with a fork.

Serve chicken over the rice and garnish with toasted sesame seeds and fresh mint (optional).

Savory Ginger Chicken Thighs and Drumsticks

This recipe is similar to Vietnamese Gà Kho Gùng, but much easier to make. It's a perfect combination of sweet and savory flavors, and will become a family favorite.

Servings: 4

Ingredients
4 to 5 lbs chicken thighs and drumsticks
2 red onions, quartered
¼ cup chicken stock
¼ cup soy sauce
1 tbsp fish sauce
2 tbsp honey
½ tbsp olive oil
2 tbsp brown sugar
½ tsp, red pepper flakes
1 (3-inch) piece ginger, cut in very thin julienne strips
4 garlic cloves, chopped
1 tsp Chinese five-spice blend
1 tsp white pepper
2 shallots, minced
Zest of 1 lemon
Juice of 1 lemon
1 lemon, sliced
1 tbsp unsalted butter
1 to 3 tsp flour

How to make it
Preheat the oven to 425° F.

Pat the chicken dry with paper towels and set aside.

In a large bowl, whisk together the chicken stock, soy sauce and fish sauce, honey, olive oil, brown sugar, red pepper flakes, ginger, garlic, Chinese five-spice, white pepper, shallots and the lemon zest and juice. Pour mixture into a large, sealable, plastic bag or an airtight container. Add the chicken and toss to coat well. Place in a refrigerator for at least 30 mintues.

Spray a 9-by-13-inch baking dish with baking spray, then place the chicken in the dish and arrange the lemon slices and red onion in between the pieces of chicken.

Roast for 25 to 35 minutes, basting halfway through, until the chicken is tender and the internal temperature reaches 165° F.

Remove from oven and transfer the chicken, lemon slices and onions to a serving platter.

Pour the cooking liquid through a sieve into a small saucepan. Discard solids. Bring to a boil over medium-high heat. Combine flour and 2 tbsp of cold water in a small bowl. Add flour mixture and butter to sauce, stirring with a whisk until blended. Return to a low boil. Cook for 1 minute or until sauce thickens, stirring constantly.

Pour the sauce over the chicken and serve.

Coconut-Peanut Curry Chicken

Coconut milk and peanut butter-flavored with a little spicy kick of red curry makes this one creamy and delicious dish. It's awesome served with white rice.

Servings: 4

Ingredients
2 tbsp olive oil
4 large boneless, skinless, chicken breasts, cut into bite-sized pieces
1 yellow onion, chopped
1 red bell pepper, seeded and cut into ¼-inch strips
1 red green pepper, seeded and cut into ¼-inch strips
1 tsp white pepper
1 tsp ground ginger
4 tbsp yellow curry powder
2 tbsp red curry paste
¼ cup peanut butter
2 (14-oz) cans coconut milk, unsweetened
Juice of 1 lime (plus additional lime slices for serving)
1 (14-oz) can baby corn, drained (whole or cut)

GARNISH
¼ cup fresh cilantro, chopped
Lime slices

How to make it
Heat the olive oil in a large pan or skillet over medium heat. Add chicken pieces in a single layer without crowding. Cook for about 4 to 5 minutes per side or until chicken is browned; remove with tongs and set aside on a plate. Repeat with remaining chicken pieces.

In the same pot, add the onion and bell peppers and cook for 3 to 4 minutes over medium heat until the onion starts to soften. Then add the white pepper, ginger, curry powder, red curry paste, peanut butter, coconut milk and lime juice. Mix together and cook for another 5 minutes.

Return the cooked chicken along with the baby corn to the pot; stir and cook for 5 minutes.

Serve with white rice and garnish with cilantro and lime slices.

Creamy Garlic Chicken Pasta with Zucchini and Yellow Squash

Servings: 4

Ingredients

3 tbsp olive oil
12 oz tri-color rotini pasta
4 boneless, skinless, chicken breasts, cut into bite-size chunks
3 cloves garlic, minced
½ tsp salt
½ tsp black pepper
1 tsp dried oregano
1 tsp dried basil
3 tbsp butter
1 cup sliced mushrooms
1 zucchini, cut into julienne strips
1 yellow squash, cut into strips
1 cup heavy cream
1 shallot, finely chopped
Zest from 1 lemon
2 tsp fresh lemon juice
½ cup grated parmesan cheese
1 cup grated Romano cheese, divided
¼ cup fresh parsley, minced, plus some for garnish

How to make it

Cook the pasta according to package instructions until al dente. Drain and set aside.

Heat oil in a large skillet on medium-high heat, add the chicken breast chunks, followed by salt, black pepper, oregano and basil. Cook until no longer pink. Transfer the chicken from the skillet to a plate and set aside.

Add the butter and mushrooms to the skillet and sauté 10 minutes. Add in zucchini and yellow squash, and sauté for an additional minute until they become slightly translucent. Remove from heat and set aside.

Add the heavy cream, shallot and lemon zest in a saucepan. Bring to a simmer over medium-high heat (watch that it doesn't boil over), then reduce the heat and simmer for 10 minutes. Remove from the heat and stir in the lemon juice, parmesan and ½ cup of Romano cheese. Remove from heat and stir until the cheese has melted.

Add the cooked pasta and chicken to the skillet with the zucchini and squash, pour in the cheese sauce to coat, then stir in remaining Romano cheese and ¼ cup parsley. Gently mix until well combined.

Serve immediately, garnished with fresh chopped parsley.

Lemon Chicken

This was the first recipe I ever made from a cookbook. It's still one of my all-time favorites.

Servings: 4

Ingredients
MARINADE
2 lbs boneless, skinless, chicken breasts, cut into 1-inch pieces
1 egg
2 tsp cornstarch
2 tsp dark soy sauce
¼ tsp white pepper

BATTER
¼ cup all-purpose flour
¼ cup water
2 tsp cornstarch
2 tsp olive oil
¼ tsp baking soda
¼ tsp salt

½ cup grapeseed or vegetable oil (for frying)

SAUCE
2 tsp grapeseed or vegetable oil
½ cup chicken broth
¼ cup honey
¼ cup lemon juice
3 tbsp light corn syrup
3 tbsp white vinegar
3 tsp ketchup
¼ tsp salt
¼ tsp white pepper
1 tsp lemon zest
2 tbsp cornstarch

GARNISH
4 green onions, finely chopped
2 tsp sesame seeds
A few lemon slices to garnish

How to make it
In a large bowl, whisk the egg, cornstarch, soy sauce and white pepper. Add the chicken, toss well to coat, cover and refrigerate for at least 30 minutes.

Heat oil in a wok or frying pan on medium-high heat. When oil is hot, add chicken and fry in batches in a single layer for about 5 to 6 minutes, turning them over halfway during cooking, until golden and cooked through.

Transfer the cooked chicken to a paper towel-lined plate. Discard the oil and wipe wok/pan dry with paper towel.

Using the same wok/pan, add all of the sauce ingredients and heat over medium-high heat. Stir sauce until simmering and thickened. Return the chicken to the wok/pan and mix with the sauce until evenly coated (about 2 minutes).

Transfer to a serving dish and garnish with green onions, sesame seeds and lemon slices.

Serve with jasmine rice.

Slow Cooker Mojo Pork Roast

Ingredients
4-5 lbs boneless pork shoulder or pork butt
6 cloves garlic, minced
1 small shallot, minced
¼ cup olive oil
1 tsp white-wine vinegar
1 cup fresh cilantro
½ cup fresh mint leaves
¼ cup fresh oregano leaves
2 tsp ground cumin
Zest of 1 orange
Zest of 2 limes
½ cup orange juice
½ cup lime juice
¼ cup lemon juice
1½ tsp salt
1 tsp black pepper
2 tbsp of cornstarch

How to make it
Using a food processor or blender, blend together garlic, shallot, olive oil, white-wine vinegar, cilantro, mint, oregano, cumin and the orange and lime zest; pulse until everything is finely chopped.

Transfer the mixture to a mixing bowl, add the orange, lime and lemon juices, salt and pepper, and whisk together.

Set aside about ¼ cup of the mojo sauce for later and keep it in the fridge while the pork cooks.

Place the pork in the slow cooker, fat side down and pour the mojo sauce over it. Cover and cook on high for 5-6 hours or on low for 9-10 hours.

Before the pork is done, preheat oven to 425° F.

When the pork is fully cooked and tender (between 155-160° F), carefully transfer it to a baking sheet, fat side up. Leave the juices in the slow cooker. Bake the roast in a 425° F oven for 15-25 minutes until browned on top.

While the roast is browning, thicken the cooking juices by adding 2 tbsp of cornstarch. Slowly stir into the mixture, turn off the slow cooker and cover.

Once the pork has browned, remove it from the oven and let cool for 10 minutes, then pull the pork apart using two forks. Return the pulled pork to the slow cooker and mix with thickened juices.

Serve with the reserved mojo sauce drizzled over the top.

NOTE: This recipe is perfect as a mean dish served over rice, but it's also great for tacos or burritos.

Caribbean Pork Chops with Spicy Lime-Rum Jerk Sauce

I love this recipe, but the spicy heat flavor may not be for the faint of heart. One scotch bonnet pepper can be up to 40 times hotter than a jalapeño. If you like things spicy, but with much less heat, use a jalapeño instead of the scotch bonnet.

Servings: 4

Ingredients
4 pork chops, thick cut

MARINADE
½ cup olive oil
¼ cup brown sugar
1 tbsp dried, ground thyme
1 tbsp allspice
2 tsp garlic powder
1 tsp cayenne
1 tsp salt

SAUCE
1 tsp ground cloves
2 tsp allspice
2 tsp garlic powder
1 tsp ground ginger
1 tbsp dried, ground thyme
1 medium red onion, chopped
4 green onions, chopped
1 scotch bonnet pepper, seeded and chopped (or 1 jalapeño pepper)
2 tbsp white vinegar
2 tbsp soy sauce
¼ cup olive oil
¼ cup ketchup
¼ cup spiced rum
¼ cup brown sugar
Zest and juice of 1 lime
1 tsp salt
1 tsp ground black pepper
Lime wedges, for garnish

How to make it
MARINADE
Combine all of the marinade ingredients in a large resealable bag or container; add the pork chops. Place in a refrigerator for at least 4 hours or overnight. When ready to cook, remove the chops from the refrigerator and allow it to come to room temperature.

SAUCE
Place all of the sauce ingredients into a blender or food processor and purée until smooth.

Transfer the liquid to a saucepan, bring to a boil over medium-high heat. Reduce heat to low and simmer for 15 to 20 minutes, stirring occasionally. Remove for heat and set aside.

Heat 2 tsp olive oil in a grill pan or large heavy skillet over high heat. Add the chops and cook for 5 to 6 minutes on each side or until cooked through. Remove from the pan and let rest for 5 minutes before serving.

Drizzle the jerk sauce over the chops and serve with lime wedges and extra sauce on the side.

Hot Dog Skillet Casserole

I had just graduated from art school when I first heard of this recipe. At the time, I thought it didn't sound very appetizing. But I was on a budget, so I gave it a try; to my surprise it was very tasty. I've made it many times over the years. I sometimes replace the hot dogs with smoked sausage. Either way, it's a great, low-cost, comfort food.

Servings: 4 to 6

Ingredients
1 12-oz package of wide egg noodles
1 lb beef hot dogs, cut into bite-size pieces
1 medium yellow onion, chopped
3 tbsp olive oil
1 10.5-oz can cream of mushroom soup
¾ cup milk
1 14.5-oz can diced tomatoes, not drained
¼ cup parmesan cheese
1 tsp dried oregano leaves, crushed
2 tbsp parsley, chopped
½ tsp salt
1 tsp pepper

How to make it
Cook noodles according to directions on the package.

Meanwhile, in a large skillet, heat olive oil over medium-high heat, add the hot dogs and cook until they start to brown, then add the onions and sauté until opaque.

Reduce heat to low and slowly stir in the mushroom soup, milk, tomatoes, parmesan cheese, oregano, parsley, salt and pepper. Stir together until well mixed and smooth.

Drain the noodles and add to the skillet. Turn heat to medium and simmer for 5 minutes, stirring occasionally until well combined.

I like to serve it with additional parmesan cheese on the side.

Orange Marmalade Pork Chops

Servings: 2 to 4

Ingredients
4 pork chops, bone in
2 tsp extra-virgin olive oil
½ cup orange juice
2 tsp fresh lime juice
¼ cup orange marmalade
2 tsp honey mustard
4 rosemary sprigs
4 orange slices
1 medium onion, sliced
1 tsp salt
½ tsp black pepper

How to make it
Preheat oven to 425° F.

Combine orange and lime juices, orange marmalade and honey mustard in a saucepan and whisk together over medium-high heat. Bring to a boil, reduce heat, simmer uncovered for 15 to 20 minutes and stir occasionally.

Heat an oven-proof pan over medium-high heat. Add olive oil and swirl to coat the skillet. Once the oil has heated, add the pork chops to the pan and sprinkle with salt and pepper. Cook until browned (about 5 to 6 minutes). Turn pork over, add the onion and orange slices to the pan and place a rosemary sprig on top of each chop.

Pour the marmalade mixture over the pork chops and bake at 425° F for 10 to 15 minutes or until a meat thermometer registers 145° F.

Serve pork chops with a few spoonfuls of the marmalade sauce from the pan and top and decorate with orange and onion slices.

Orange-Ginger Glazed Pork Chops

Servings: 2 to 4

Ingredients

CHOPS
4 pork chops, thick cut, boneless

SAUCE
2 tbsp olive oil
¼ cup honey
¼ cup soy sauce
2 tbsp white vinegar
2 tbsp Dijon mustard
¼ cup orange marmalade
2 tbsp freshly grated ginger
¼ cup orange juice
1 tsp orange zest
2 cloves garlic, minced
1 tbsp fresh ground pepper
1 tsp cornstarch

GARNISH (optional)
4 orange slices
4 rosemary sprigs

How to make it
Preheat oven to 375° F.

In a mixing bowl, combine the honey, soy sauce, white vinegar, Dijon mustard, ginger, orange marmalade, orange juice, orange zest, garlic, fresh ground pepper and cornstarch.

Heat olive oil in a large, oven-proof skillet over medium-high heat. Add pork chops and cook for about 5 minutes on each side until browned. Pour mixture over chops, top each chop with a rosemary sprig and bake at 375° F for 10 minutes or until a thermometer registers 140°.

Remove chops, place on serving dish. Drizzle sauce over chops and garnish with orange slices.

Root Beer-Glazed Baby Back Ribs

Servings: 2 or 3

Ingredients
- 1 12-oz can root beer
- 6 oz of your favorite prepared barbecue sauce
- 2 tbsp apple cider vinegar
- ¼ cup molasses
- 2 lbs baby back ribs (about 2 slabs)

RUB
- ½ cup dark brown sugar
- 2 tbsp smoked paprika
- 1 tsp cinnamon
- 2 tbsp ground celery seed
- 1 tbsp chili powder
- ½ tsp ground allspice
- ½ tsp cayenne pepper
- 2 tbsp kosher salt

How to make it

Heat a small sauce pan to medium-high, add the soda and bring to a simmer until it is reduced by three quarters. Slowly add the barbecue sauce and vinegar.

Cook for 2-3 minutes and then remove from the heat and set it aside.

In a medium-size mixing bowl, combine all of the rub ingredients and mix well. Rub both sides of the slab of ribs with molasses. Then evenly coat the ribs with the rub.

Preheat oven to 250° F.

Wrap the ribs in non-stick aluminum foil. Place the foil-wrapped ribs on a sheet pan and bake for about 3 hours. Remove from the oven and carefully unwrap a section of the foil and test that the meat can easily be pulled from the bone. If it doesn't pull away easily, return it to the oven for about 20 to 30 more minutes.

Remove from the oven and remove the foil. Brush the slabs with the sauce.

Raise the oven temperature to 450° F. Place the ribs back in the oven, uncovered. Cook for about 10 minutes or until the sauce starts to bubble and caramelize.

Using a sharp knife, slice the ribs into portions between the bones and serve with additional sauce on the side.

Rosemary-Dijon Pork Chops

Servings: 4

Ingredients
4 bone-in pork chops
½ cup honey
¼ cup Dijon mustard
2 tbsp chopped, rosemary (fresh or dried)
2 garlic cloves, minced
2 tbsp olive oil
½ tsp salt
½ tsp pepper

How to make it
In a small bowl, mix together the honey, mustard, rosemary, garlic, olive oil, salt and pepper.

Place the pork chops in a resealable container or a large freezer bag and pour the marinade over the chops. Make sure all of the chops are covered with the marinade. Seal the container and place it in the fridge for at least two hours or overnight.

Remove the container from the refrigerator and let stand for 10 to 15 minutes before cooking. (Meat at room temperature cook more evenly.)

Grill the pork chops on medium-high heat for 5 to 6 minutes on each side or until the center of the meat is no longer pink.

Remove from the grill and rest for 5 minutes on a plate covered in foil before serving. This allows juices to be distributed throughout the meat.

San Francisco Pork Chops

Servings: 4 to 6

Ingredients
6 boneless pork chops, with fat trimmed off
2 tbsp olive oil

SAUCE
2 tsp olive oil
1 garlic clove, minced
4 tbsp dry sherry or beef broth
4 tbsp soy sauce
3 tbsp brown sugar
¼ tsp crushed red pepper
2 tsp cornstarch
2 tbsp water

How to make it
Heat olive oil in a skillet over medium heat. Brown chops in hot oil, about 5 minutes per side; remove pork to a platter, reserving oil in the skillet.

Add the garlic to the reserved drippings and sauté for about one minute. In a large bowl, whisk the sherry or broth, soy sauce, brown sugar, two tsp olive oil and red pepper.

Return pork chops to skillet and pour the sauce mixture over the chops. Bring sauce to a boil, cover skillet and reduce heat to low. Simmer chops until tender, 30 to 35 minutes, turning once halfway through cooking. If needed, add 1 to 2 tbsp of water to keep the sauce from cooking down too much.

Transfer chops to a platter. Whisk cornstarch and water in a small bowl until smooth; stir into pan juices and simmer until thickened, about 5 minutes.

Pour sauce over chops and serve.

This is great served with egg noodles, pasta with butter and sauce or mashed potatoes.

Pork Tenderloin with Seared Pears and Shallots

Servings: 4

Ingredients

4 tbsp olive oil
2 garlic cloves, finely chopped
1 tbsp fresh thyme, chopped, plus extra for garnish
½ tsp kosher salt
½ tsp black pepper
3 shallots, quartered
3 unpeeled Bosc or Anjou pears, cored and quartered (note: you will need a total of 4 pears: 3 to cook with the pork and 1 for the sauce)
1½ lb pork tenderloin
4 sprigs rosemary

SAUCE
1 unpeeled Bosc or Anjou pear, cored and quartered
1 tbsp unsalted butter
1 tbsp all-purpose flour
½ tsp brown sugar
½ tsp ground cinnamon
¼ tsp ground allspice
½ cup chicken broth
½ tsp vanilla extract

How to make it

Preheat oven to 475° F.

In a small bowl, combine olive oil, garlic, thyme, salt and pepper, then rub mixture over the pork, shallots and 3 pears.

Heat a large, nonstick skillet over medium-high heat. Add the pork and cook until brown on all sides, about 6 to 7 minutes.

Transfer the pork to a baking sheet, lined with foil (do not clean the skillet). Roast the pork until thermometer inserted into its center registers 145° F, about 10 to 12 minutes. Allow pork to rest for at least 10 minutes.

Meanwhile, add the pears and shallots to the skillet and cook over medium-high heat until they start to brown, turning once or twice. Transfer to a platter and set aside.

SAUCE
Add the all of the sauce ingredients to a high-speed blender or food processor. Process until smooth.

Transfer the mixture to a sauce pan and heat on medium-high until a low boil starts; reduce heat to low and cook for 5 minutes.

Slice the pork and arrange on a platter with pears and shallots. Drizzle sauce over the pork and sprinkle with thyme.

Caribbean-Spiced Pork Tenderloin with Pineapple-Mint Salsa

Servings: 4

Ingredients
SALSA
1 cup frozen or fresh pineapple, chopped
1 red bell pepper, seeded and chopped
1 jalapeño pepper, seeded and chopped
¼ cup red onion, finely chopped
2 tbsp fresh mint, finely chopped
1 tsp garlic, minced
1 garlic clove, minced
1 tbsp brown sugar
Salt and pepper to taste

1 lb pork tenderloin
2 tbsp olive oil (plus more for browning)
2 tbsp lime juice
2 tsp soy sauce
3 tbsp Caribbean jerk seasoning
1 tsp dried rosemary, crushed
½ tsp salt

How to make it
SALSA
Place all of the salsa ingredients into a small bowl, mix well and set aside.

In another small bowl, combine the olive oil, lime juice, soy sauce, jerk seasoning, rosemary and salt. Pour the mixture into a large, sealable, plastic bag or an airtight container. Add the tenderloin and toss to coat well. Place in a refrigerator for at least 30 mintues.

Preheat the oven to 400° F.

Remove the pork from the marinade.

Lighty coat a cast iron grill pan or oven-safe skillet with olive oil. Heat the oil over medium-high. Brown the tenderloin for about 4 minutes on each side.

Transfer to the preheated oven and roast for 20 to 30 minutes or until the internal temperature is 145° F.

Remove from oven, place the pork on a cutting board and let it rest for 10 minutes before carving.

Cut into thin slices, top with the salsa and serve immediately. I like to serve it with white rice.

Roasted Pork Loin with Apples, Pears and Prunes

This tasty and elegant main dish is easy to throw together. Plated with the apples, pears, prunes and red onions makes a stunning presentation. I like to refer to this recipe as fruit bowl pork.

Servings: 8

Ingredients
1 (3 to 4 lbs) boneless pork loin roast, trimmed
4 cloves garlic, minced
2 tsp kosher salt
½ tsp freshly ground black pepper
3 tbsp olive oil, divided
¼ cup brown sugar
2 tbsp all-purpose flour
2 tbsp unsalted butter, melted
¼ cup balsamic vinegar
1½ cup beef broth
2 large tart cooking apples (such as Granny Smith or Honeycrisp), quartered
3 Bosc pears, each cut into 8 wedges
1¼ cup dried, pitted prunes, chopped
1 large red onion, cut into quarters
3 to 4 fresh rosemary sprigs
3 fresh sage leaves

How to make it
Preheat the oven to 400° F. Adjust the oven rack to the middle position. Remove the pork loin from the refrigerator and let it rest while the oven is heating.

In a small bowl, mix the garlic, black pepper and kosher salt. Gradually stir in enough olive oil to form a thick paste.

Pat the pork dry with paper towels. Rub the entire pork loin with the garlic mixture. Set aside at room temperature for 30 minutes.

Heat olive oil in a large cast iron pan or heavy skillet over medium-high heat until shimmering. Add the pork and sear on all sides until it's deep golden-brown and easily releases from the pan, (about 4 to 6 minutes per side). Once all sides have browned, turn off the heat and set aside.

Stir the brown sugar and flour together in a mixing bowl, whisk in the melted butter, balsamic vinegar and the beef broth.

Arrange the apples, pears, prunes, onion, rosemary and sage in a roasting pan. Drizzle with the balsamic vinegar and beef broth mixture.

Nestle the browned pork loin on top of the apples, pears, prunes, onion, rosemary and sage, and pour in any accumulated juices from the skillet.

Place in preheated oven and roast until an instant-read thermometer inserted into the thickest part of the pork reads 145° F (about 1 hour).

Remove the pan from the oven and transfer the pork to a cutting board. Let the pork loin rest for 15 to 20 minutes before slicing.

Serve the sliced pork with the apples, pears, prunes and onion pieces. Drizzle with some of the pan drippings.

Black-Eyed Peas with Sausage, Ham Hocks and Bacon

This recipe is comfort food at its highest. Black-eyed peas are a symbol of luck and have become a New Year's tradition in the South. For the best of luck, eat them anytime of the year. I love serving them over rice with collard greens on the side.

Ingredients
1 lb black-eyed peas, dry
1 large smoked ham hock
1 large yellow onion, chopped
6 cups chicken broth
2 bay leaves
½ tsp dried thyme
½ tsp cayenne pepper
1 (12-oz package) smoked pork sausage, sliced
8 slices bacon, chopped
1 onion, diced
2 ribs celery, diced
1 carrot, peeled and chopped
1 green bell pepper, diced
2 cloves garlic, minced
1 (10-oz can) diced tomatoes with chilies
Salt and pepper to taste

How to make it
Rinse black-eyed peas and remove any debris. Place in a large bowl, soak beans overnight, covered by at least 2 inches of water.

Drain the black-eyed peas and place in a large pot along with the ham hock, onion, chicken broth, bay leaves, thyme and cayenne pepper. Bring to a boil over medium-high heat. Reduce heat to a simmer, cover and cook for 1 hour.

Meanwhile, cook the chopped bacon in a frying pan until it's crisp. Remove bacon and place on a paper towel-lined plate. Add the sliced sausage, onion, celery, carrot, bell pepper and garlic to the pan with the bacon grease and cook on medium-high heat until the sausage is lightly browned on both sides. Remove from heat and set aside.

Once the pot with the black-eyed peas and ham hock has simmered for a full hour, transfer the ham hock from the pot to a cutting board. When cool enough to handle, discard skin and bones, chop the meat, and return meat to the pot along with the sausage and onion mixture, bacon and the can of tomatoes (undrained), stir well and simmer for 15 more minutes.

Remove and discard the bay leaves from the pot and season with salt and pepper if needed.

Serve over cooked rice directly from the pot using a slotted spoon.

Lamb Chops with Garlic-Mint Sauce

These lamb chops make for an elegant dish and are surprisingly easy to make. The garlic-mint sauce can be made ahead of time and stored in the refrigerator for up to 1 month. The sauce also goes great with grilled chicken.

Servings: 4

Ingredients
MINT AND GARLIC SAUCE
1 cup fresh mint, finely chopped
½ cup fresh parsley leaves, finely chopped
1 cup olive oil
3 cloves garlic, minced
2 tsp white wine vinegar
1 tsp lemon zest
1 tbsp fresh lemon juice
½ tsp red chili flakes
½ tsp salt

LAMB
2 tbsp olive oil
8 Frenched rib lamb chops
1 tsp salt
1 tsp pepper

How to make it
Combine all of the sauce ingredients together in a bowl and whisk well. Refrigerate until ready to use.

Heat oil in a grill pan or large heavy skillet over high heat until it's almost smoking. Generously season lamb chops with garlic, salt and pepper on both sides.

Grill lamb chops in batches if necessary. Add the chops to the hot grill pan and sear for 3 to 4 minutes, flip them over and cook for another 3 minutes for medium-rare or 4 minutes for medium.

Place the cooked chops on a platter and let them rest for 5 minutes prior to serving. Generously drizzle each with garlic-mint sauce.

Serve with extra sauce on the side.

Herb-Crusted Lamb Chops with Raspberry Sauce

These succulent herb-crusted lamb chops, drizzled with sweet raspberry sauce, make a beautiful presentation and the flavor is poetic. I drool just thinking about them.

Servings: 2

Ingredients
SAUCE
½ cup red wine (Cabernet or Merlot)
2 cups fresh raspberries
½ cup raspberry jam
2 tsp fresh thyme leaves, finely chopped
¾ cup sugar
½ tsp salt

LAMB CHOPS
Canola oil for frying (or other oil with a high smoke point)
8 to 10 lamb chops, Frenched
¼ cup Dijon mustard
½ cup seasoned breadcrumbs
2 tsp fresh thyme leaves, finely chopped
1 tsp fresh rosemary leaves, finely chopped
2 tsp fresh mint leaves, chopped
2 tsp garlic powder
1 tsp freshly ground black pepper
½ tsp salt

Raspberries, rosemary sprigs and chopped mint, for garnish

How to make it
SAUCE
Place all of the sauce ingredients into a blender or food processor and purée until smooth.

Transfer the liquid to a saucepan, bring to a boil over medium-high heat. Reduce heat to medium-low and simmer until the sauce is reduced and thickens, about 30 minutes. Stir occasionally and watch so it doesn't burn. Remove from heat and set aside.

LAMB CHOPS
Remove the lamb chops from the refrigerator and let sit, covered, to come to room temperature, about 30 minutes.

In a shallow bowl, mix together the breadcrumbs, thyme, rosemary, mint, garlic, black pepper and salt.

Pat the lamb chops dry with paper towels. Brush all sides of each chop with Dijon mustard, then roll in breadcrumb mixture until well-coated. Tap off any excess.

Heat 3 tbsp oil in cast iron or stainless steel skillet over medium-high heat. Place half of the lamb chops in the pan and cook until golden brown, about 3 minutes per side. Remove from pan and repeat with remaining lamb chops and oil.

Transfer the chops to serving plates, drizzle the raspberry sauce around or over the chops and garnish with raspberries, rosemary sprigs and mint leaves.

Burrowing Owl

SEAFOOD

Sesame-Crusted Tuna with Mango Salsa

Servings: 4

Ingredients

MANGO SALSA
2-3 ripe mangos, diced
1 red bell pepper, seeded and diced
½ red onion, diced
1 jalapeño, seeded and minced
¼ cup cilantro leaves, chopped
2 limes
½ tsp salt

SESAME-CRUSTED TUNA
4 ahi tuna steaks (1½ to 2 inches thick, about 6 oz each)
¼ cup white sesame seeds
¼ cup black sesame seeds
Salt and pepper
1 tbsp olive oil

How to make it

Add mango, red pepper, red onion, jalapeño and cilantro to a medium-size bowl and mix together.

Squeeze lime juice over the top and sprinkle with salt and stir.

Refrigerate until ready to serve.

Season the tuna on both sides with salt and pepper.

Press the tuna into the sesame seeds, coating completely on all sides.

Heat the oil in a skillet over medium-high heat. To avoid overcrowding the pan, sear two tuna steaks at a time. Use tongs to gently support the steaks while searing. Once the pan is hot, sear each side just long enough for the white sesame seeds to develop a little golden color, 1 to 1½ minutes per side.

Transfer the tuna to a cutting board, repeat the process with the remaining steaks.

Cut the tuna steaks into thin slices and arrange over fresh greens.

Serve with mango salsa and steamed rice.

Coconut Shrimp with Orange Sauce

Ingredients

COCONUT SHRIMP
1 lb raw jumbo shrimp, peeled and deveined
Olive oil for frying
2 eggs
¼ cup cornstarch
¾ cup Panko bread crumbs
1 cup unsweetened, shredded coconut
1 pinch salt and black pepper

ORANGE SAUCE
½ cup orange marmalade
2 tsp honey mustard
⅛ tsp crushed red chili flakes
2 tsp lime juice
1 pinch salt

How to make it

In a small bowl, combine all sauce ingredients and whisk well. Cover and place in refrigerator until ready to serve.

If using frozen shrimp, thaw according to package directions. Raise the shrimp and pat dry with paper towels.

You will need 1 shallow bowl and 2 medium mixing bowls. Whisk the eggs in the shallow bowl and set aside. Combine cornstarch, salt and pepper in one medium bowl. Mix bread crumbs and coconut in the third bowl.

One at a time, dip each shrimp into the cornstarch, then the eggs, and then the coconut mixture. I like to use a lot of coconut. Dredge the shrimp with the coconut mixture and press gently to adhere. Place on a baking sheet, repeat with remaining shrimp.

Add enough olive oil to cover the bottom of a large skillet on medium heat. Fry the shrimp in batches of 4 to 5, until golden brown on both sides, about 3 to 4 minutes per batch. Place cooked shrimp on a plate lined with a paper towel as you fry the rest.

Plate and serve with the orange sauce drizzled on top or on the side for dipping.

Air frying method: Preheat the air fryer to 330° F. Place shrimp in the fryer basket without overcrowding and cook for about 10 to 15 minutes per batch.

Lump Crab Cakes with Chipotle Sauce

Makes: 6 crab cakes

Ingredients

CRAB CAKES
1 egg
¼ cup mayonnaise
2 tbsp sweet onion, finely minced
2 tbsp red bell pepper, finely chopped
2 tbsp fresh parsley, finely minced
2 tsp Dijon mustard
2 tsp Worcestershire sauce
1 tsp Old Bay seasoning
¼ tsp cayenne powder or more if you like a spicier kick
1 tsp fresh lemon juice, plus more for serving
¼ tsp kosher salt
1 lb pasteurized lump crab meat, drained
⅔ cup saltine cracker crumbs

CHIPOTLE SAUCE
½ cup mayonnaise
1 tsp puréed or ground chipotle pepper
1 tsp finely chopped cilantro
1 tsp ground cumin
½ tsp kosher salt, or to taste
½ tsp freshly ground black pepper
1 tsp fresh lime juice

How to make it

To make the chipotle sauce, place all ingredients in a blender or food processor. Blend on high speed until smooth and creamy. Place in an airtight container and refrigerate until ready to serve.

To make the crab cakes, whisk the egg, mayonnaise, onion, red bell pepper, parsley, Dijon mustard, Worcestershire sauce, Old Bay, cayenne powder, lemon juice and salt together in a large bowl. Add the crab meat and cracker crumbs, and gently mix together with a rubber spatula or large spoon. Be careful not to break up the crab meat.

Cover the boxing bowl tightly and refrigerate for at least 30 minutes and up to 1 day.

Preheat oven to 425° F. Grease a baking sheet with olive oil or nonstick spray.

Using an ice cream scoop or a ½ cup measure, scoop out 6, ½ cup mounds of the mixture on the baking sheet. Leave a 2" space between each mound. Gently compact each individual mound so there are no lumps sticking out. Do not flatten the mounds.

Bake for 15-20 minutes or until lightly browned around the edges and on top.

Squeeze fresh lemon juice over each cake and serve warm with chipotle sauce.

Southern Shrimp and Cheesy Grits

Servings: 4

Ingredients
3 cups chicken broth
½ cup heavy cream
2 tsp salt
1½ cups corn grits
4 tbsp butter
2 cups cheddar cheese, shredded
1 tsp freshly ground black pepper
8 slices slab bacon
1 lb large shrimp, peeled and deveined
3 garlic cloves, minced
1 tsp smoked paprika
1 tsp ground cayenne pepper
1 red bell pepper, finely chopped
4 green onion, thinly sliced, plus more for garnish
1 tbsp Worcestershire sauce
1 tsp Tabasco sauce
Juice of 1 lemon
3 tbsp parsley chopped

How to make it
In a medium saucepan, bring the broth and heavy cream to a boil and season with salt.

Reduce heat to medium, so broth is at a simmer. Whisk in the grits and lower the heat to medium-low. Cover and simmer for about 40 to 60 minutes, stirring occasionally.

Once the grits are cooked, stir in the butter, cheese and black pepper. Remove from heat and cover.

Meanwhile, in a large skillet over medium heat, cook bacon until crispy, about 7 to 8 minutes. Reserve about 3 tbsp of bacon fat in skillet. Transfer the cooked bacon to a paper towel-lined plate. Once the bacon has cooled, crumble it into small pieces and set aside.

Place the shrimp in a bowl and season with garlic, smoked paprika and cayenne pepper. Toss the shrimp so they are evenly coated with the seasoning.

Reheat the skillet, add the shrimp, bell pepper and green onions. Cook, stirring occasionally, until shrimp is pink and cooked through, about 4 to 5 minutes. Stir in Worcestershire, Tabasco and lemon juice.

Spoon desired amount of warm grits on 4 serving plates or bowls. Make a well in the center and fill it with the shrimp mixture and top with crumbled bacon. Garnish with the reserved green onions and chopped parsley.

Coconut Curry Soup with Shrimp and Mussels

This is my favorite recipe in this entire book; it's as yummy as it looks and is easy to make.

Servings: 4

Ingredients
8 oz wide lo mein noodles
14-oz can of coconut milk
32 oz chicken stock
1 small white or yellow onion, cut in quarters
3 cloves of garlic
1 tsp fresh or ground ginger
1 medium jalapeño pepper, seeded and chopped
4 tbsp red curry paste
¼ cup cilantro leaves, finely chopped, divided
2 limes, juiced
1 tsp soy sauce
½ tsp kosher salt
½ tsp white pepper
1 red bell pepper, seeded and julienned
2-lb bag frozen mussels
½ lb jumbo shrimp, pre-cooked, peeled, deveined, tail on
4 green onions, finely chopped

How to make it
Cook the lo mein noodles according to the directions on the package.

Place the coconut milk, onion, garlic, ginger, thai chili pepper, red curry paste, ½ of the cilantro leaves, lime juice, soy sauce, salt and white pepper in a blender. Blend until the ingredients are well combined and completely smooth.

Heat a large pot to medium heat and add the chicken stock and the red bell pepper, then pour in the mixture from the blender. Let everything simmer for about 10 to 15 minutes. While that is simmering, cook the mussels according to directions. I use a microwave for this. Add the cooked mussels and the shrimp to the soup.

In 4 bowls, place in the cooked lo mein noodles and then top with the soup mixture. Garnish with the remaining cilantro and green onions.

Rice Noodles with Shrimp and Coconut-Lime Dressing

Servings: 4

Ingredients
¼ cup sweetened coconut milk
1 tsp finely grated lime zest
Juice from the two limes
4 tsp fish sauce
1 shallot, finely chopped
1 tbsp brown sugar
¼ cup olive oil
½ tsp kosher salt
8 oz wide lo mein rice noodles
12 jumbo shrimp, peeled, cooked and deveined
1 English cucumber, sliced thin
1 red bell pepper, seeded and sliced thin
1 cup fresh cilantro leaves
1 jalapeño, seeded and finely chopped
¼ cup crushed, salted, roasted peanuts

How to make it
Place the coconut milk, lime juice, fish sauce, shallot, brown sugar, olive oil and salt in a blender and blend until smooth and emulsified. Place in a covered container and chill in refrigerator until ready to use.

Toss shrimp, cucumber, red bell peppers, cilantro and jalapeño in a large bowl with three-quarters of the dressing to combine and evenly coat, and set aside.

Cook rice noodles according to package instructions. Drain and rinse under cold water. Divide the noodles into 4 serving bowls.

Divide and place the shrimp and vegetable mixture on top of the noodles and drizzle the remaining dressing over the top. Garnish with peanuts and serve.

Jambalaya with Shrimp and Sausage

Servings: 4 to 6

Ingredients

4 tbsp olive oil, divided
1 lb cooked andouille or kielbasa sausage, sliced into rounds
1 white onion, diced
2 ribs celery, diced
1 large red bell pepper, seeded and diced
1 medium jalapeño pepper, seeded and chopped
4 cloves garlic, peeled and minced
14 oz crushed tomatoes
3½ cups chicken stock
1½ cups long-grain white rice
2 tbsp Cajun seasoning
1 tsp dried thyme, crushed
½ tsp cayenne pepper
1 lb raw large shrimp, peeled and deveined
½ tsp kosher salt
1 tsp freshly ground black pepper
¼ cup freshly squeezed lemon juice

Optional garnishes: chopped parsley or thinly sliced green onions

How to make it

Heat 2 tbsp olive oil in an 8- to 12-qt. stock pot or large Dutch oven over medium heat. Add sausage and sauté until lightly browned, about 5 minutes. Transfer sausage to a plate and set aside.

Add remaining 2 tsp olive oil to the pot. Add onion, celery, bell peppers, jalapeño and garlic to the pot. Sauté until vegetables are softened, stirring occasionally, about 5 minutes.

Add tomatoes, chicken stock, rice, Cajun seasoning, thyme, cayenne pepper and sausage to the pot and stir to combine. Bring to a simmer and reduce heat to low, cover and simmer for about 25-30 minutes, or until the rice is nearly cooked through, stirring every 5 to 7 minutes along the way so that the rice does not burn.

Remove lid and add shrimp. Stir to incorporate the shrimp into the rice and continue cooking until shrimp are pink and just cooked through, about 5 minutes. Season to taste with salt, pepper and additional Cajun seasoning if desired. Remove from heat.

Serve warm with your desired garnishes.

Grilled Ahi Tuna Steak with Bing Cherry Salsa

Servings: 4

Ingredients

TUNA STEAKS
4 6-8 oz Ahi tuna steaks
2 tbsp olive oil
2 tbsp lemon juice
1 garlic clove, minced
Kosher salt and cracked black pepper to taste

CHERRY SALSA
1 cup bing cherries, pitted and chopped
1 cup cherry tomatoes, halved
¼ cup red onion, finely chopped
1 cup cucumber, finely chopped
1 jalapeño, seeded and finely chopped
½ cup cilantro, finely chopped
2 tbsp fresh lime juice
½ tsp olive oil
½ tsp ground coriander
Kosher salt and cracked black pepper to taste

How to make it

CHERRY SALSA
Add all of the ingredients for the cherry salsa into a bowl and mix until well blended. Refrigerate for at least 30 minutes.

TUNA STEAKS
In a large, sealable, plastic bag or bowl with a locking lid, combine the lemon juice, olive oil and garlic. Add the tuna steaks and seal. Refrigerate for 30 to 45 minutes, turning occasionally.

Heat a cleaned grill to high and season it with oil to ensure the fillets don't stick.

Sprinkle steaks with salt and pepper, and grill each side for 2 to 3 minutes. The center should be raw and lukewarm to the touch, or the tuna will be tough and dry.

Let the tuna rest for 5 to 10 minutes; serve topped with the cherry salsa.

NOTE: The salsa is also delicious with grilled chicken breasts, pork chops or simply served with tortilla chips.

Rosemary Salmon with Caramelized Oranges

Servings: 4

Ingredients
CARAMELIZED ORANGES
4 oranges, large and sweet
½ cup granulated sugar
¼ cup water
1 tsp ground cinnamon
½ tsp vanilla extract
2 tbsp orange juice

ROSEMARY SALMON
4 skinless salmon fillets
2 tbsp olive oil
1 garlic clove, minced
4 tbsp orange juice
1 tbsp honey
½ tbsp finely chopped fresh rosemary leaves
1 tsp cornstarch
1 tsp salt
½ tsp pepper
4 rosemary sprigs for garnish

How to make it
Peel oranges to the flesh using a paring knife, then slice oranges into ½ inch-thick slices. Arrange the slices on plates and sprinkle with cinnamon and set aside.

In a saucepan, combine the water, vanilla extract, orange juice and sugar. Bring to a boil over medium heat and allow the caramel to color a bit, about 5-10 minutes.

Remove the saucepan from the heat and let cool for 2 to 3 minutes. Add the orange slices to the pan, stir the caramel over the slices and set aside.

Brush the top of the salmon with olive oil and sprinkle with salt and pepper.

Heat large, cast iron or non-stick skillet on medium heat. Add the salmon to the hot pan and sear for 2-3 minutes.

Add the orange juice, garlic and rosemary.

Once the one side has seared, flip it over and sear the other side for 2-3 minutes or until done to your liking.

Divide and arrange the caramelized oranges on four serving plates.

Flip the salmon before serving and place over the caramelized oranges, drizzle remaining sauce over the top and garnish with rosemary sprigs. I like to serve it with white rice.

Lobster Stuffed with Crab Imperial

Servings: 4

Ingredients
4 (16 to 20 oz) lobster tails
16 oz lump crab meat
½ cup mayonnaise
1 tsp sugar
1 tsp parsley, finely chopped
¼ cup freshly squeezed lemon juice
1 tsp Worcestershire sauce
2 tsp Old Bay seasoning
2 eggs, lightly beaten
½ cup sharp cheddar cheese, shredded
¼ cup unsalted butter, melted
Lemon wedges for serving

How to make it
Preheat oven to 425° F.

In a large bowl, mix the mayonnaise, sugar, parsley, lemon juice, Worcestershire sauce, Old Bay seasoning, eggs and the cheddar cheese.

Add the lump crab meat to the mixture and gently toss, making sure not to break up the large pieces of crab meat.

Using kitchen shears, carefully cut the back shell of each lobster tail from front to back lengthwise.

Pull the edges of the split lobster shells apart and gently lift the tail meat to rest above the shells. Place the prepared lobster tails on a baking sheet.

Brush the lobster meat with melted butter. Evenly divide the stuffing and top each lobster tail. Gently press stuffing mixture into the tops so it doesn't fall off.

Bake for 15-20 minutes. Lobster is done when a thermometer inserted into the heart of the meat reads 140 to 145 degrees. Do not overcook.

Serve with lemon wedges.

Pan-Seared Salmon with Creamy Cilantro Lime Sauce

Servings: 4

Ingredients
4 skinless salmon fillets (4-6 oz)

RUB
2 tsp ground cumin
1 tsp ground coriander
½ tsp onion powder
½ tsp cayenne pepper
½ tsp salt
1 tsp freshly ground black pepper
1 tbsp olive oil

SAUCE
½ cup sour cream or greek yogurt
2 green onions, roughly chopped
½ cup fresh cilantro
Juice of 1 lime
Zest of 1 lime
1 clove garlic, minced

Lime wedges for serving

How to make it
SAUCE
Add all ingredients to a high-speed blender or food processor. Purée until cilantro has been very finely minced.

Chill in the refrigerator while preparing salmon.

FOR THE SALMON
Combine all of the rub ingredients in a mixing bowl.

Pat all sides of salmon dry with paper towels. Generously season both sides of the fillets with the rub mixture.

Heat the olive oil in a 12-inch nonstick skillet over medium-high heat until hot and shimmering. Cook the salmon, top side down first, until golden and crisp, about 4 minutes. Carefully flip the fillets and reduce the heat to medium. Continue cooking for about 4 minutes more or until done to your liking.

Transfer to a platter and serve with creamy cilantro lime sauce and lime wedges.

Seafood Paella

Servings: 6

Ingredients
4½ cups chicken broth
2 tbsp fish sauce
1 tsp lemon juice
½ tbsp saffron threads, crumbled (optional)
3 sprigs fresh thyme
2 tbsp smoked paprika
3 tbsp olive oil
1 yellow onion, finely chopped
1 red or yellow bell pepper, seeded and diced
3 cloves garlic, thinly sliced
8 oz Spanish chorizo or andouille sausage, sliced
3 cups short-grain rice, such as bomba, calasparra or arborio
1 (14-oz) can roasted, diced tomatoes
1 lb clams, such as littlenecks, cleaned
1 lb mussels, cleaned
1 lb large shrimp, peeled and deveined, with tails left on
3 lobster tails, halved lengthwise
1½ cup frozen green peas
¼ cup chopped parsley, for garnish
2 lemons, cut into wedges for serving

How to make it
Preheat the oven to 400° F.

Add the chicken broth, fish sauce and lemon juice to a saucepan and heat over medium high; bring to a boil. Add the saffron and thyme sprigs. Turn off the heat and let steep for 15 to 20 minutes.

Remove and discard the thyme sprigs from the broth mixture.

Toss the shrimp with the smoked paprika and set aside.

In a Dutch oven or large, oven-safe stock pot, heat the oil over medium heat. Add the onion, bell pepper and garlic, cook until the onion is translucent (about 5 to 8 minutes). Add the sausage and rice, and cook until slightly browned (about 3 to 5 minutes).

Pour in the broth mixture and the diced tomatoes; stir until combined. Bring to a simmer, then nestle the clams and mussels into the rice with the hinge sides up so they release their juices into the rice. Cover and let simmer for 5 minutes.

Add the shrimp and lobster. Cover and place in the perheated oven for 25 to 30 minutes, until the clams and mussels are opened.

Remove from oven and place the pot back on the stove over medium-high heat. Add the peas. Cook until the bottom of the rice forms a light crust, about 5 minutes. Watch out not to over-cook and burn.

Discard any clams or mussels that remain tightly shut once everything else has been cooked.

Sprinkle with parsley and serve with lemon wedges.

Pan-Seared Scallops with Lemon Caper Sauce

Servings: 4

Ingredients
1 lb large or jumbo scallops
Fine sea salt
3 tbsp grapeseed (or other high smoke point oil)
1 tbsp unsalted butter
1 tbsp minced garlic
½ cup white wine
1 cup chicken broth
12-oz container cherry or grape tomatoes
8-oz container baby bella mushrooms, sliced
Zest of 1 lemon
Juice of 1 lemon
3 tbsp capers
2 tbsp Dijon mustard
2 tbsp fresh dill, chopped
2 tbsp fresh chives, chopped
2 lemons, cut into wedges

How to make it
For the best browning results, it's crucial to remove as much surface moisture as possible. Arrange the scallops in a single layer on the paper towel-lined plate. Gently pat the top of the scallops with paper towels.

Preheat a 12-inch cast iron skillet or sauté pan over medium-high heat. When the pan is hot, add the grapeseed oil.

Sprinkle scallops lightly with salt on both sides. Carefully place scallops into the hot pan without crowding. Sear undisturbed until golden brown (about 2 to 3 minutes). Scallops should release easily from the pan. If not, let them cook a little longer.

Reduce heat to medium and add butter. Turn each scallop over with a spatula or metal tongs. Use a large spoon and baste the scallops with the melted butter and cook for another 1 or 2 minutes.

When the center of the scallops are opaque and firm to the touch, remove from the pan and set aside.

Using the same pan, add the garlic and sauté for 1 minute. Increase heat to medium-high and add wine, tomatoes and mushrooms. Simmer until tomatoes begin to burst and release juices (about 4 to 5 minutes).

Increase heat to high, add the chicken stock, lemon zest and juice, capers and Dijon mustard to the pan. Cook until sauce is reduced by half (about 8 to 10 minutes).

Reduce heat to medium and return the scallops to the pan, cook until warm (about 2 minutes).

Garnish with chopped dill, chives and lemon wedges.

Caribbean White Fish in Curry Sauce

If you like seafood and curry, you will love this recipe. You can use any firm white fish like cod, grouper, haddock or flounder. This super tasty and healthy meal is simple to prepare and goes well with rice.

Servings: 2 to 4

Ingredients
4 large skinless white fish fillets
Juice of 1 lemon
2 tbsp curry powder, divided
1 tsp white pepper
1 tbsp olive oil
1 yellow onion, chopped
2 tbsp ginger, finely grated
2 garlic cloves, minced
1 jalapeño, seeded and finely chopped
1 red bell pepper, chopped into chunks
1 tsp thyme leaves, chopped
1 (14-oz can) coconut milk
1 tsp parsley, chopped (optional)

How to make it
Place the fish fillets in a shallow dish and drizzle with lemon juice and sprinkle with 1 tbsp of curry powder and the white pepper; set aside while you make the sauce.

Heat the olive oil in a large cast iron pan or deep frying pan over medium-high heat until shimmering. Add the onion, ginger, garlic, jalapeño and bell pepper, and sauté for 5 minutes, then stir in the remaining curry powder and thyme, and cook for another minute.

Add the coconut milk and simmer, uncovered, for 10 minutes until the sauce has thickened.

Add the fish, gently push the fillets down into the sauce, then cover the pan with a lid and lightly simmer for 8-10 minutes or until the fish flakes easily.

Garnish with parsley and serve.

Rich and Creamy Lobster Pot Pie

This lobster pot pie is decadent and delicious. Served as a main dish with a salad and some crusty bread makes for a perfect meal for a date night. To make things easy, I typically use store-bought puff pastry, frozen vegetables and frozen, pre-cooked lobster.

Servings: 4

Ingredients
6 tbsp unsalted butter
3 cloves garlic, minced
2 russet potatoes, washed and diced
1 large yellow onion, chopped
20 oz frozen vegetables (I like to use a combo of corn, carrots and green beans)
¼ cup bourbon (optional)
1 cup seafood stock
1 cup heavy cream
3 tbsp all-purpose flour, plus more for rolling out the puff pastry
1½ lb pre-cooked lobster meat, chopped
½ tsp cayenne powder
½ tsp dried tarragon
1 tsp dried rosemary
Salt and freshly ground black pepper to taste
1 sheet puff pastry, thawed
1 egg, beaten

How to make it
Melt butter in a skillet over medium-high heat. Add garlic and potatoes. Cook for 10 minutes. Add the onion, frozen vegetables, bourbon and seafood stock, and bring to a low boil.

Gently whisk the flour and heavy cream. Cook, stirring constantly, until the sauce is slightly thickened, (about 4 to 5 minutes). Stir in lobster, cayenne, tarragon, rosemary, salt and pepper.

Preheat oven to 400° F.

Spray a 12-inch oval baking dish with cooking spray. Pour the filling into the baking dish and set aside.

On a lightly floured surface, roll pastry into a flat sheet, large enough to cover the baking dish. Place the puff pastry over the dish and press to seal it tight around the edges. Cut four small vents into the top of each pastry.

Brush pastry with the egg and bake until golden on top, about 30 minutes. Serve hot.

Two or Three Leagues

Pastas and Pizza

Baked Ziti with Sausage and Peppers

Servings: 6

Ingredients

SAUSAGE AND PEPPERS
3 tbsp olive oil
1¼ lbs Italian sausage (sweet or hot)
1 onion, thinly sliced
4 cloves garlic, minced
3 bell peppers (red, green and yellow), seeded and cut into thin strips
24-oz jar of your favorite pasta sauce
2 tsp Italian seasoning
Salt and freshly ground pepper to taste

BAKED ZITI
12 oz ziti pasta
24-oz jar of your favorite pasta sauce
2 eggs, lightly beaten
15 oz ricotta cheese
2½ cups shredded mozzarella cheese
½ cup grated parmesan cheese plus more for garnishing
2 tsp Italian seasoning
¼ cup fresh basil leaves, finely chopped plus more for garnishing
Salt and freshly ground pepper to taste

How to make it

SAUSAGE AND PEPPERS
In a large skillet with a lid, heat olive oil over medium-high heat. Add sausages and onion; cook, turning the sausages to brown on all sides and onions are tender, about 10 minutes. Add garlic and bell peppers, and cook another five minutes.

Add pasta sauce, Italian seasoning, salt and pepper. Increase heat to high and cook until liquid starts to boil. Reduce heat to medium-low, cover and simmer until the sausages feel firm; about 25 minutes. Cut the sausages into slices before serving.

BAKED ZITI
Heat oven to 350° F.

Bring a large pot of lightly salted water to a boil. Add ziti pasta and cook according to package's directions until al dente. Drain, rinse under cold water and set aside.

Mix the remaining ziti ingredients in a large bowl. Add pasta and mix lightly. Spoon into a 13 x 9-inch baking dish, sprayed with cooking spray.

Bake uncovered for 30 minutes or until it's lightly browned and bubbling around the edges.

Remove from heat and let rest about 10 to 15 minutes before cutting through it. Serve topped with sausage and peppers, and sprinkled with additional fresh parmesan cheese and chopped basil.

Italian Sausage and Spinach Gnocchi

This recipe is quick, easy, flavorful and delicious. It makes a complete and hardy meal. Serve it with fresh Italian baguettes and your family or guests will be in food heaven.

Servings: 4 to 6

Ingredients
2 tbsp olive oil
2 (19 oz) packages Italian sausage, hot or mild
1 medium yellow onion, chopped
3 cloves garlic, minced
½ cup chicken stock
1 can 14.5 oz diced tomatoes
1 can 6 oz tomato paste
1 tsp thyme
1 tsp dried rosemary
1 tsp dried parsley flakes
½ tsp salt
½ tsp black pepper
1 (16 oz) package gnocchi
1 (16 oz) package fresh baby spinach
½ cup mozzarella cheese, shredded
½ cup parmesan cheese, shredded
2 tbsp fresh thyme, chooped

How to make it
Place the uncooked sausage in the freezer for 15-20 minutes; this will make slicing it much easier.

Preheat oven to 425° F.

Once the sausage is firm, transfer it to a cutting surface and slice at a 45-degree angle to your desired thickness and set aside.

Add the olive oil to a large, oven-safe skillet and heat stove top to medium-high.

Once the oil is hot, add in the chopped onion and stir until transparent. Stir in the garlic.

Add the sausage, cover with the lid and cook until lightly browned or about 8-10 minutes.

Remove lid and add in the chicken stock, undrained diced tomatoes, tomato paste, thyme, rosemary, sage, parsley flakes, salt, pepper and the gnocchi. Stir until well combined.

Stir in the spinach, making sure it's covered with liquid.

Add the mozzarella and parmesan cheese and stir until well combined.

Place in the oven and bake for 25 minutes.

Remove from the heat, garnish with thyme and serve it while it's hot.

Creamy Cajun Chicken Alfredo with Smoked Sausage

This recipe is creamy, cheesy and loaded with flavor, and can be made in less than 30 minutes! I like to make it with penne pasta, but fettuccine or virtually any other favorite pasta works just as well.

Servings: 6

Ingredients
2 tbsp olive oil
2 boneless, skinless, chicken breasts, cut into bite-size pieces
1 (12-oz) package Cajun-style andouille smoked sausage, sliced
1 tbsp Cajun or Creole seasoning
½ tsp onion powder
1 tsp oregano
½ tsp crushed red pepper flakes
4 tbsp unsalted butter
3 cloves garlic, minced
2 tbsp flour
2 cups heavy cream
1 cup chicken broth
2 cup fresh mini-San Marzano or cherry tomatoes
2 cup shredded Italian five-cheese blend or shredded parmesam cheese
6 oz fresh baby spinach
½ tsp freshly ground black pepper
2 tbsp fresh parsley, chopped
16 oz penne pasta

How to make it
Cook the pasta according to package instructions until al dente. Drain and set aside.

Heat the olive oil in a large pan or skillet over medium heat. Add sausage in a single layer without crowding. Cook for about 4 to 5 minutes per side, until the sausage starts to brown. Stir in the chicken and sprinkle with the Cajun seasoning, onion powder, oregano and red pepper flakes. Cook until the chicken is no longer pink and is cooked through (about 5 to 7 minutes).

Remove the sausage and chicken from the pan and set aside.

In the same skillet, add the butter and garlic, sauté for 30 seconds or until fragrant. Mix in the flour and cook for 2 minutes.

Whisk in the heavy cream and chicken broth. Add the tomatoes and bring to a simmer. Cook for 3 minutes then add the cheese and stir until well combined.

Reduce heat to low, add the spinach and cook until wilted. Return the chicken and sauge to the pan and mix well.

Add the cooked penne pasta to the skillet and toss to coat.

Sprinkle with parsley and serve hot.

Individual Pizza Pot Pies

This recipe is inspired by the pizza pot pie made legendary at the Pizza and Oven Grinder Company in Chicago. Besides being delicious, the best part is you can customize each individual pizza. Or better yet, make a pizza bar of various toppings on your kitchen countertop and have your family and friends create their own. You can make it easy with store-bought pizza sauce and dough or make it from scratch. I go the easy way.

Servings: 4

Ingredients
16 oz pizza dough, quartered, pulled and stretched into 4, 10-inch circles
15 oz pizza sauce
6 oz tomato paste
16-oz package sliced mozzarella cheese
Your favorite pizza toppings
1 tsp olive oil

How to make it
Preheat oven to 400° F.

Mix the pizza sauce and tomato paste together in a small bowl and set aside. The paste makes the sauce thicker and helps to keep the filling combined and not runny when you flip the pies.

Spray bottoms, sides and rims of 4 (10-oz) oven-safe bowls or ramekins with cooking spray.

Line entire bowl with mozzarella; make sure it is completely covered. Add pizza fillings, cover with sauce mixture. Each bowl should be filled up to its rim.

Cover each bowl with dough. Brush the top of the dough with olive oil.

Place bowls on a baking sheet and bake until crust is golden (about 20 to 30 minutes).

Once fully cooked, remove from oven and let cool for 10 minutes,

Turn over onto plates. Remove bowls and serve.

Bacon Cheeseburger Lasagna

Servings: 8

Ingredients
2 lbs ground beef
2 cups yellow onion, diced
2 tbsp garlic, minced
15 oz tomato sauce
½ cup ketchup
3 tbsp yellow mustard
1 lb bacon, cooked and crumbled
1 lb lasagna noodles
1 egg
15 oz ricotta cheese
1 cup Monterey jack cheese, shredded
1 cup sharp cheddar cheese, shredded
1 tsp kosher salt
1 tsp black pepper
½ cup dill or bread and butter pickle slices, if desired

OPTIONAL TOPPINGS
Fresh tomatoes, diced
Shredded iceberg lettuce
Dill or bread and butter pickle slices
Additional ketchup and mustard

How to make it
Spray 13" x 9" baking dish with cooking spray. Set aside.

In a large skillet, cook the ground beef, onion and garlic over medium-high heat for 5 to 7 minutes, stirring frequently, until beef is brown; drain. Stir in tomato sauce, ketchup and mustard, and the crumbled bacon. Simmer for 5 minutes, stirring occasionally.

Meanwhile, in medium-size bowl, whisk the egg and stir in the ricotta and Monterey jack cheese, salt and pepper; mix well and set aside.

Spread 1 cup beef mixture over bottom of baking dish. Top with 4 uncooked noodles. Spread half of the cheese mixture over noodles; top with 1½ cups beef mixture. Add a single row of pickles (if desired). Repeat layers again with 4 noodles, remaining cheese mixture and 1½ cups beef mixture. Top with remaining 4 noodles, beef mixture and 1 cup cheddar cheese.

Cover with foil and refrigerate for at least 8 hours or overnight.

Heat oven to 350° F. Bake covered, 45 minutes. Remove from oven, uncover and bake 25 to 35 minutes longer or until bubbly.

Remove from oven. Cover with foil and let stand for 10 to 15 minutes before cutting.

Serve with optional toppings if desired.

King of the Everglades

Desserts and Sweets

Blueberry and Lemon Bread Pudding

Servings: 6

Ingredients
2½ cups heavy cream
2 tbsp unsalted butter
3 eggs
¼ cup sugar
2 tsp vanilla bean paste or extract
22-oz can lemon pie filling
5 to 6 cups of day-old bread, torn into 2-inch pieces
1 cup blueberries

How to make it
Preheat the oven to 350° F.

Heat the cream and butter in a medium saucepan until the butter has melted, then set aside.

In a medium-size bowl, whisk together the eggs, sugar and vanilla, until well combined. Slowly add the cream and butter mixture while continuing to whisk.

Butter a 12- by 9-inch baking dish. Spoon about ¼ cup of lemon pie filling into the bottom. Add a layer of bread cubes and blueberries, and half of the remaining lemon pie filling. Add another layer of bread cubes and blueberries, and dollop the remaining lemon pie filling. Pour the cream mixture on top.

Bake at 350° F for 30 to 40 minutes, or until mixture begins to bubble at the edges. Remove from oven and allow to rest for 5-10 minutes. I like to serve it warm.

Tip: You can also make this in individual ramekins.

Apple Dumplings

Makes: 6 dumplings

Ingredients
SAUCE
2 cups sugar
2 tsp cinnamon
1 tsp nutmeg
2 cups water
1 tsp vanilla bean paste or extract
2 tbsp butter

DUMPLINGS
6 sweet-tart baking apples
1/3 cup chopped walnuts
1/3 cup raisins or chopped dates
1/3 cup light brown sugar
2½ cups all-purpose flour
2 tsp baking powder
½ tsp salt
½ cup vegetable shortening, cut into cubes
½ cup warm milk
2 eggs

How to make it
Preheat oven to 350° F.

Combine all of the sauce ingredients in a medium-size saucepan over medium-high heat, stirring to dissolve sugar. Bring to a full boil stirring constantly. Reduce heat to medium and continue to boil for 5 minutes, stirring constantly. Remove from heat and set aside.

Peel and core all the apples. Make sure you get all the seeds out. Set aside.

In a small bowl, mix the walnuts, raisins and brown sugar. Set aside.

In another small bowl, whisk the 2 eggs and set aside.

In a medium-size bowl, whisk together flour, baking powder and salt. Add the cubes of shortening and use your fingers to mix the dough. Add heated milk and stir, using a fork, until dough begins to hold together.

Divide dough into 6 equal pieces and using a rolling pin, one at a time, roll each piece of dough approximately 6" square. Place apple on pastry; fill cavity with nut mixture. Brush edges of pastry with the whisked eggs. Bring the opposite corners to the top of the apple and press seams together.

Place each dumpling in a large baking dish. Pour sauce around dumplings and transfer to oven; bake for 45 minutes or until dumplings are golden brown and sauce is bubbling.

Serve warm in bowls with the hot syrup that's in the bottom of the baking dish and vanilla ice cream or whipped cream, if desired.

Chocolate Raspberry Tart

Makes: 1, 9-inch tart

Ingredients

CRUST
1½ cups graham crackers
¼ cup unsweetened cocoa
¼ cup light brown sugar
½ tsp kosher salt
6 tbsp unsalted butter, melted

GANACHE
8 oz dark chocolate baking chips
8 oz milk chocolate baking chips
1 cup heavy cream
1 cup butter, softened
2 tbsp instant coffee

TOPPING
16 oz prepared caramel topping
3 cups fresh raspberries

How to make it

Preheat the oven to 350° F and grease a 9-inch tart pan.

Pulse the graham cracker in a food processor until finely ground.

Transfer to a bowl and add the cocoa and melted butter. Mix until thoroughly combined.

Press the mixture evenly into the tart pan. Bake for 6 minutes. Remove from the oven, cool and chill for 20 to 30 minutes.

Place all of the chocolate chips in a large bowl. Set aside.

In a small saucepan, bring the heavy cream and butter to a low boil. Add the instant coffee and pour the hot mixture into the bowl over the chocolate chips.

Let the mixture stand for 2 minutes and then mix thoroughly until smooth.

Pour the chocolate ganache into the graham cracker crust and smooth out the top with a spatula.

Place in the refrigerator and let set for about 2 hours.

Once completely set, cover the ganache with the caramel and smooth out the top with a spatula, then decorate with fresh raspberries.

Keep refrigerated until ready to serve.

Appeltaart: Dutch Apple Pie

Makes: 1, 9-inch pie

Ingredients

CRUST
2 cups all-purpose flour
1 cup dark brown sugar
½ tsp salt
2 cups unsalted butter, chilled and cubed
1 egg

FILLING
7 large tart apples (I use Granny Smith)
1 cup raisins, soaked in water
1 tbsp ground cinnamon
¼ cup brown sugar
¼ cup granulated sugar
1 tbsp grated ginger
Juice of one lemon
2 tsp rum extract
2 tbsp all-purpose flour

FINISH (optional)
¼ cup apricot jam
1 tbsp sparkling sugar

How to make it

CRUST
In a large bowl, mix the flour, brown sugar and salt together. Add the butter and the egg and work it into the flour until it starts to resemble bread crumbs. Knead the dough until smooth; form it into a ball and wrap it in plastic wrap and place it in the refrigerator for at least 20 minutes.

FILLING
Put the raisins in a small bowl, add enough water to cover them, let them soak for 20 to 30 minutes and set aside until needed.

Peel and core the apples and cut them into cubes and place in a bowl. Drain the water from the raisins and add them to the bowl. Add the cinnamon, brown sugar, granulated sugar, ginger, lemon juice, rum extract and the flour. Stir well to combine.

Preheat your oven to 350° F.

Coat a 9-inch springform pan with baking spray.

Take ⅔ of the dough and roll it out on a well-floured counter and line the bottom of the springform pan as well as up the sides.

Place the apple filling into the dough-lined pan.

Decorate the top of the pie with the remaining dough by rolling it into 1-inch strips and creating a lattice pattern.

Place the pie into the oven and bake for 60 minutes.

Remove from the oven and while the pie is still hot, brush apricot jam on the top to create a glossy finish, then sprinkle with sparkling sugar.

Bananas Foster

Bananas Foster originated at Brennan's Restaurant in New Orleans in the early 1950s. Owen Brennan asked his chef Paul Blangé to create a banana-based dessert. It's been a staple dish at the restaurant ever since. It was named for Richard Foster, the chairman of the New Orleans Crime Commission and a good friend of the restaurant owner.

This delightful dessert is surprisingly easy to make and will impress every guest at your dinner table.

Servings: 4

Ingredients
4 bananas, peeled and cut in half lengthwise, then halved
½ cup unsalted butter
1 cup brown sugar
1 tsp cinnamon
¼ cup dark rum
¼ cup banana liqueur
Vanilla ice cream, for serving

How to make it
Melt the butter in a large skillet over medium-high heat. Add the brown sugar and cinnamon, and cook until color deepens, about 3 to 4 minutes.

Add bananas, cut-sides down. Cook for 3 minutes and carefully flip the bananas; cook for an additional 3 minutes.

Turn the burner off and add the rum and banana liqueur. Use a stick lighter to ignite the alcohol. Cook until flames die out, about 20 to 30 seconds.

Plate the bananas with a scoop or two of vanilla ice cream. Generously spoon warm sauce over the top and serve immediately.

Peanut Butter Cheesecake with Chocolate Graham Cracker Crust

This delectable cheesecake is one of my all-time favorite desserts. It's so good and worth every calorie.

This recipe is very easy to make, but if you want to make things even easier, use two, 9-inch, store-bought (ready for baking) graham cracker pie crusts. The filling in this recipe is enough to fill both. If you use this method, reduce the baking time to 45 to 60 minutes.

Makes: 1, 9-inch cheesecake

Ingredients
CRUST
1¼ cup graham cracker crumbs
⅓ cup butter, melted
⅓ cup unsweetened cocoa powder
⅓ cup sugar

FILLING
3 (8-oz packages) cream cheese, softened
4 eggs
2 tsp vanilla extract
1½ cups sugar
1 (10-oz package) peanut butter chips

CHOCOLATE DRIZZLE
½ cup semi-sweet chocolate chips
1 tbsp shortening (do not substitute with oil or butter; it has to be shortening or it will not harden)

How to make it
Preheat oven to 350° F.

Lightly spray a 9-inch springform pan with baking spray.

Crush the graham crackers into crumbs in a plastic bag with a rolling pin or in a food processor. Mix with melted butter, cocoa powder and ⅓ cup sugar. Press crust mixture into the bottom of the springform pan and set aside.

In a large bowl, beat the softened cream cheese and 1½ cup of sugar until smooth. Gradually beat in eggs and vanilla, then add the peanut butter chips; mix until well combined. Add eggs and vanilla; beat well. Pour the filling over the crust.

Bake 60 to 70 minutes or until the center is almost set. Remove from oven. With knife, loosen cake from the side of the pan. Cool for 20 to 30 minutes. Remove side of springform pan.

In a microwave-safe bowl, combine chocolate chips and shortening. Microwave on high for 45 to 60 seconds, stirring every 15 seconds, until chocolate is shiny and almost melted. Stir until smooth. Using a fork or spoon, randomly drizzle the melted chocolate over the top of the cheesecake. Store covered in refrigerator.

Arroz con Dulce (Puerto Rican Rice Pudding)

Arroz con Dulce is a transitional staple in Puerto Rico during Christmas. The name translates to "sweet rice" which perfectly describes this yummy dessert. In recent years, it's been served year-round in many restaurants and cafes on the island.

Servings: 8

Ingredients
1½ cup medium or short-grain rice
4 cups water
3 cinnamon sticks
1 tsp whole cloves
1 (2-inch) piece fresh ginger, peeled
¼ cup brown sugar
¼ tsp ground nutmeg
½ tsp salt
1 (15-oz can) cream of coconut
¾ cup raisins
Ground cinnamon, for garnish

How to make it
In a medium-size bowl, add rice and enough water to completely cover the rice. Let rice soak between 3 hours to overnight.

In a Dutch oven or large saucepan over medium-high heat, bring 4 cups of water to a boil, add the cloves, ginger, cinnamon sticks, brown sugar, nutmeg and salt. Lower heat to medium-low; simmer for 10 minutes. Using a slotted spoon, remove and discard spices. Do not discard the water.

Drain the rice and add it to the Dutch oven. Stir in the cream of coconut and raisins. Return heat to high and bring to a boil.

Lower heat to a low simmer, covered, until rice is soft and liquid is absorbed (about 15-20 minutes). Stir every 5 minutes. Remove from heat and let cool to room temperature. Pour the Arroz con Dulce into a container or dish and cover, and refrigerate until chilled.

If the pudding seems dry after refrigerating, stir in a little milk.

To serve, scoop pudding onto small serving plates or bowls and sprinkle with ground cinnamon.

Mom's Date Nut Pudding

My mother's date nut pudding has been a family Christmas tradition for many years. As a kid, I wasn't a fan of the topping and would scrape it off and replace it with more whipped cream. Today, I absolutely love the topping, but still wonder why it's called pudding, when it's more like a cake. This recipe is moist, chewy, nutty and very rich; a small serving can be very filling. My mother would slice it into 24 smaller serving sizes. It's divine served warm with a dollop of whipped cream.

Servings: 12

Ingredients
DATE NUT PUDDING
1 cup dates, pitted and finely chopped
1 cup boiling water
1 tsp baking soda
1 cup sugar
1 tbsp butter
1 egg, beaten
1 tsp baking powder
1 tsp vanilla
1 cup all-purpose flour
½ cup walnuts chopped

TOPPING
1 cup dates, pitted and finely chopped
1½ cup sugar
¾ cup water
1 cup walnuts, chopped (divided)
Whipped cream

How to make it
Preheat oven to 375° F.

DATE NUT PUDDING
Spray an 8- or 9-inch square or round baking dish with non-stick baking spray.

Place the chopped dates, sugar and butter in a medium-size saucepan and bring to a boil.

Place the chopped dates into a mixing bowl and pour the boiling water over the dates. Add the baking soda, stir occasionally and let set until cooled.

When cool, add the sugar, butter, egg, baking powder, vanilla and flour, and mix to combine. Stir in the walnuts until well combined.

Pour the batter into the prepared baking dish and bake until a toothpick inserted into the center of cake comes out clean, about 30 to 40 minutes. Let it cool for at least 10 minutes before adding the topping; it needs to be firm.

TOPPING
Place 1 cup of chopped dates, 1½ cup sugar and ¾ cup of water in a medium saucepan and bring to a boil. Boil until the mixture thickens and turns in color. Stir in ½ cup chopped walnuts, remove from heat and let cool.

Once the pudding and topping has cooled, spread the topping evenly over the pudding, then sprinkle the remaining ½ cup chopped walnuts over the top.

Serve with a dollop or two of whipped cream.

Chocolate Marshmallow Bread Pudding

Servings: 8 to 10

Ingredients
2 large whole eggs
3 egg yolks
1 cup sugar
4 cups chocolate milk
1 tsp instant coffee (optional)
1 tsp vanilla extract
1 tsp unsalted butter, melted
1 loaf day-old French bread, cut or torn into 1-inch pieces
8-to-10-oz package semi-sweet chocolate chips
16-oz jar marshmallow fluff
Chocolate syrup (optional topping)

How to make it
Place the eggs and yolks into a blender and combine on the low speed for 30 seconds. Add the sugar, chocolate milk, instant coffee, vanilla and melted butter, and blend on low until incorporated, about 30 seconds.

Spray a 9 x 13-inch baking dish with cooking spray.

Arrange the bread pieces evenly in a baking dish and top with the chocolate chips.

Slowly pour the milk mixture over the bread and chips. Press the bread into the mixture with a spatula so it's thoroughly saturated.

Set aside at room temperature for 30 minutes.

Preheat the oven to 325° F.

When heated, marshmallow fluff will expand, so place a sheet pan on a lower oven rack, just in case anything overflows.

Bake for 30 minutes, then remove from oven and top the pudding with dollops of marshmallow fluff. Using a spatula, spread the marshmallow evenly.

Return to oven and bake for 15 additional minutes.

After baking for 15 minutes, set the oven to the broil setting. WARNING: MARSHMALLOW CAN BURN EASILY, SO WATCH CLOSELY AS IT BROWNS. THIS SHOULD TAKE LESS THAN A MINUTE.

Remove from oven, cool for 15 minutes before serving. Serve topped with chocolate syrup.

Individual Pineapple Upside-Down Cakes

Servings: 6

Ingredients
6 canned pineapple slices
6 tbsp unsalted butter
1 cup light brown sugar
6 maraschino cherries
3 large eggs
2 cups sugar
1 cup olive oil
1 cup sour cream
1 tsp vanilla extract
1½ tsp nutmeg
½ tsp salt
2½ cups all-purpose flour
1 tsp baking powder
1 tsp baking soda

How to make it
Preheat the oven to 350° F.

Spray 6 ramekins with baking spray.

In a small saucepan, melt the butter over medium heat. Stir in the brown sugar and cook until the sugar has dissolved.

Evenly spoon the brown sugar mixture into the ramekins. Place a maraschino cherry in the center of each pineapple slice and set aside.

In a large bowl, whisk the eggs and sugar until well combined. Stir in the olive oil, sour cream and vanilla extract until its smooth. Add the nutmeg, salt, flour, baking powder and baking soda, and mix well.

Spoon the cake batter over each pineapple, until two-thirds full.

Bake for 30 to 35 minutes or until a toothpick inserted in the center comes out clean.

Cool on a rack for 5 minutes. Then run a knife around the edges of the ramekins.

Invert the cakes onto dessert plates and serve.

Very Berry Pie

I like to get a little creative when baking pies. I use cookie cutters to make fun shapes out of the top layer of crust. For patriotic holidays I use star shapes. Heart shapes can be used for Valentine's Day and snowflakes or candy cane shapes are perfect for Christmas. To make things easy, I use premade pie crust.

Servings: 8

Ingredients
14-oz box premade, refrigerated pie crust, 2 count
2 cup fresh raspberries
2 cup fresh blackberries
4 cup fresh blueberries
1 cup sugar
3/8 cup cornstarch
1 tsp lemon juice
1 tsp milk

How to make it
Heat oven to 400° F.

Spray a 9-inch pie dish with baking spray. Place 1 pie crust into the dish and press firmly against the side and bottom.

In a large bowl, gently mix berries, sugar, cornstarch and lemon juice.

Spoon the berry mixure into crust-lined pie dish. Add the second pie crust to the top and press edges together to seal. Cut slits in several places of the top crust. Or if using cutout shapes, arrange them over the top. Brush with milk and sprinkle with sugar.

In case of potential spillovers, place the pie on a foil-lined baking sheet. Place on the middle rack of oven and bake 45 to 55 minutes or until the filling is bubbly and the crust is golden brown.

Remove from the oven and cool for at least 3 hours. I prefer to let the pie rest overnight at room temperature, as the filling will set up and not run. Refrigeration can result in the filling collapsing and pulling away from the crust.

Fire Ride

Baked Goodies

Banana Walnut Bread

Yield: 1 loaf

Ingredients
1½ cups all-purpose flour
⅔ cup granulated sugar
1 tsp baking powder
1 tsp baking soda
¼ tsp salt
1 tsp ground cinnamon
¼ tsp ground allspice
2 cups bananas, mashed (about 4 large ripe bananas)
⅓ cup unsalted butter, melted
1 large egg, beaten
1 tsp vanilla extract
¾ cup walnuts, chopped

How to make it
Preheat oven to 350° F and lightly grease a 9-by-5-inch loaf pan; set aside.

To a large mixing bowl, whisk together flour, sugar, baking powder, baking soda, salt, cinnamon and allspice.

Mix in the melted butter, sugar, egg and egg yolk, sour cream and vanilla. Add mashed bananas and stir until combined.

Fold in the chopped walnuts and transfer to the prepared loaf pan.

Bake until a toothpick comes out clean, about 45-55 minutes. Let cool for 10 minutes in pan, then remove from pan and cool on wire rack.

Cinnamon Apple Scones

Makes: 6 to 10 scones

Ingredients
2 cups all-purpose flour, plus more for dusting
2½ tsp baking powder
2 tsp ground cinnamon
1 tsp sugar
½ tsp salt
1 egg
½ cup unsalted butter, cold
½ cup heavy cream (plus some for brushing)
¼ cup applesauce (I buy the 6-packs with the individual, 4-oz cups)
½ cup light or dark brown sugar
1 tsp vanilla extract
1 cup tart apple, peeled and chopped (I like to use Granny Smith)
White coarse sugar, for topping

How to make it
Adjust oven rack to lower-middle and preheat oven to 400° F.

Line a baking sheet with parchment paper and set aside or use a nonstick scone pan.

Combine flour, baking powder, cinnamon, sugar, salt and the egg in a large bowl and mix until coarse and crumbly. (You could also use a stand mixer for this).

Cut the cold butter into small pieces and add to the flour mixture and mix until the mixture is coarse and crumbly with no pieces of butter left larger than the size of a pea.

Add the heavy cream, applesauce, brown sugar, vanilla and the chopped apples; mix well until everything appears moistened. Use a spatula or your hands to form the dough into a soft ball.

Generously dust your working surface with flour. Transfer the dough and shape into a rectangle, about ¾-inch thick. Place the dough on a sheet of parchment paper and refrigerate for 15 to 20 minutes.

With a sharp knife, cut dough into 6 triangles and arrange on the parchment-lined baking sheet or place in a scone pan.

Sprinkle with coarse sugar and bake until puffed and golden, about 30 to 35 minutes.

Blueberry-Lemon Scones

It's believed that scones originated in Scotland in the early 1500s. They were originally made with oats and griddle-baked; today's versions are made with flour and baked in the oven.

The American version is sweet, a little dry, crumbly, usually triangular shaped and contains various kinds of fruits. They are heavenly with a cup of morning or mid-day coffee or tea. This recipe is inspired by the first one I ever tried, many years ago at the Gazebo Inn in Ogunquit, Maine.

If you make them often, I highly recommend investing in a nonstick scone pan.

Makes: 6 to 10 scones

Ingredients
2 cups all-purpose flour, plus more for dusting
1 tbsp baking powder
2 tsp sugar
1 tsp salt
¼ cup olive oil
1 egg
1 cup fresh blueberries
1 tbsp fresh lemon zest
1½ tsp fresh lemon juice
14-oz can coconut milk, unsweetened

GLAZE
3 tbsp powdered sugar
1 tsp fresh lemon juice

How to make it
Adjust oven rack to lower-middle and preheat oven to 400° F.

Line a baking sheet with parchment paper and set aside or use a nonstick scone pan.

Combine flour, baking powder, sugar, salt, olive oil and the egg in a large bowl and mix until coarse and crumbly. (You could also use a stand mixer for this).

Gently fold in the blueberries, lemon zest and juice. Stir in coconut milk, mix well with a spatula to form a soft dough.

Generously dust your working surface with flour. Transfer the dough and shape into a rectangle, about ¾-inch thick. Place the dough on a sheet of parchment paper and refrigerate for 15 to 20 minutes.

With a sharp knife, cut dough into 6 triangles and arrange on the parchment-lined baking sheet or place in a scone pan.

Bake until puffed and golden, about 30 to 35 minutes.

Meanwhile, in a small bowl, combine the powdered sugar with lemon juice to make the glaze.

Allow scones to cool for about 10 minutes before drizzling with the glaze.

Mango Bread

Yield: 1 loaf

Ingredients
2 cups all-purpose flour
2 tsp baking soda
1 tsp baking powder
2 tsp ground cinnamon
½ tsp salt
½ cup unsalted butter, melted
¼ cup vegetable oil
1 cup granulated sugar
3 eggs, beaten
1 tsp vanilla
½ cup walnuts, chopped
½ cup raisins
2 cups mango, finely chopped (approximately three mangos)

How to make it
Preheat oven to 350° F. Grease a 9-by-5-inch loaf pan.

In large bowl, stir together the flour, baking soda, baking powder, cinnamon and salt until it's fully combined.

In smaller bowl, mix together the melted butter, oil and sugar until well blended.

Beat in the eggs until fully incorporated, then stir in the vanilla.

Add wet ingredients to flour mixture and stir until combined.

Add walnuts, raisins and mango to batter and fold in gently.

Pour the batter into a greased loaf pan; let stand for 15 minutes, then bake for 45 minutes to 1 hour. Do a toothpick test; if it comes out clean, it's done.

Remove from heat onto a wire rack, let cool.

Serve on its own or spread with butter if desired.

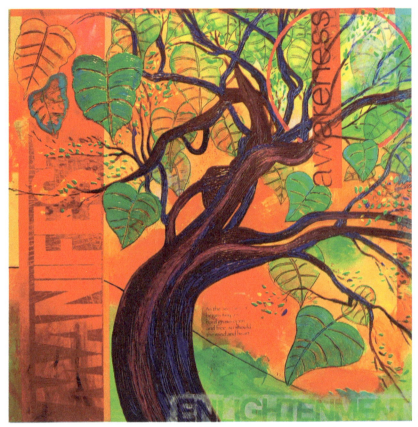
Bohi Tree

Index

A
Appeltaart: Dutch Apple Pie 228
Apple Dumplings 224
Arroz con Dulce (Puerto Rican Rice Pudding) 234
Artichoke Chicken with Bow Tie Pasta 130
Asian-Style Pepper Steak 114
Asparagus Bisque 48
Avgolemono (Greek Lemon Chicken Soup) 54

B
Bacon Cheeseburger Lasagna 218
Bacon-Kale Egg Breakfast Muffins with Sun-Dried Tomatoes 26
Baked Mashed Potatoes 74
Baked Ziti with Sausage and Peppers 210
Bananas Foster 230
Banana Walnut Bread 246
Beer-Battered Fried Pickles with Spicy Ranch Dressing 18
BEEF
  Flank Steak with Avocado Chimichurri Sauce 106
  Palomilla Steak 108
  Stir-Fried Beef and Vegetables 110
  German Sauerbraten 112
  Asian-Style Pepper Steak 114
  Mshikaki Steak Kebabs with Tomato Onion Sauce 116
  Philly Steak Mac and Cheese 118
  Rich and Creamy Beef Stroganoff 120
  Irish Shepherd's Pie with Beef Tenderloin Tips 122
Black-Eyed Peas with Sausage, Ham Hocks and Bacon 170
Bloody Mary Shrimp and Pasta Salad 70
Blueberry and Lemon Bread Pudding 222
Blueberry-Lemon Scones 250
BREAD
  Banana Walnut Bread 246
  Mango Bread 252
BREAD PUDDING
  Blueberry and Lemon Bread Pudding 222
  Chocolate Marshmallow Bread Pudding 238
Buttery, Crispy, Parmesan-Herbed Potato Stacks 86

C
Caribbean Beef Pepperpot Stew 38
Caribbean Burgers with Tropical Fruit Salsa 96
Caribbean Coconut-Curry Sweet Potato Soup 50
Caribbean Conch Fritters with Orange Aioli 14
Caribbean Pork Chops with Spicy Lime-Rum Jerk Sauce 150
Caribbean-Spiced Pork Tenderloin with Pineapple-Mint Salsa 166
Caribbean White Fish in Curry Suace 204
CRAB
  Lump Crab Cakes with Chipotle Sauce 182
CHEESECAKE
  Peanut Butter Cheesecake with Chocolate Graham Cracker Crust 232
CHICKEN
  Spicy African Chicken Peanut Stew 40
  Avgolemono (Greek Lemon Chicken Soup) 54
  Lime Chicken with Blueberry Bourbon Sauce 124
  Papaya Chicken Curry with Coconut Rice 126
  Chicken Piccata 128
  Artichoke Chicken with Bow Tie Pasta 130
  Sesame-Ginger Chicken 132
  Firecracker Chicken 134
  Tequila-Lime Chicken Tacos with Creamy Cilantro-Jalapeño Sauce 136
  Coconut Pineapple Chicken with Coconut Rice 138
  Savory Ginger Chicken Thighs and Drumsticks 140
  Coconut-Peanut Curry Chicken 142
  Creamy Garlic Chicken Pasta with Zucchini and Yellow Squash 144
  Lemon Chicken 146
Chocolate Marshmallow Bread Pudding 238
Chocolate Raspberry Tart 226
Cinnamon Apple Scones 248
Classic German Red Cabbage (Rotkohl) 90
Coconut Curry Soup with Shrimp and Mussels 186
Coconut-Peanut Curry Chicken 142
Coconut Pineapple Chicken with Coconut Rice 138
Coconut Shrimp with Orange Sauce 180
Creamy and Cheesy Sausage Potato Soup 52
Creamy Cajun Chicken Alfredo with Smoked Sausage 214
Creamy Garlic Chicken Pasta with Zucchini and Yellow Squash 144
Creamy Potato Mushroom Soup 46
CURRY
  Caribbean Coconut-Curry Sweet Potato Soup 50
  Papaya Chicken Curry with Coconut Rice 126
  Coconut-Peanut Curry Chicken 142
  Coconut Curry Soup with Shrimp and Mussels 186
  Caribbean White Fish in Curry Sauce 204

D
Date Nut Pudding 236
Dumplings (Apple) 224
Dutch Apple Pie 228
Dutch Baby Pancake with Blackberries and Sliced Almonds 32

E
EGGS BENEDICT
Eggs Benedict with Prosciutto 28
Smoked Salmon Eggs Benedict with Pan-Seared Tomatoes and Asparagus 30

F
Festive Fondant Potatoes 78
Firecracker Chicken 134
FISH
Seafood Paella 200
Caribbean White Fish in Curry Suace 204
Flank Steak with Avocado Chimichurri Sauce 106
French Onion Soup 44
Fried Green Tomatoes with Spicy Remoulade Sauce 12

G
German Roasted Purple Potato Salad 58
German Sauerbraten 112
German Spätzle/Spaetzle (Tiny Egg Noodle Dumplings) 82
Grilled Ahi Tuna Steak with Bing Cherry Salsa 192
Gyro-Inspired Greek Lamb Burgers with Tzatziki Yogurt 98

H
Ham and Cheese Casserole with Hash Brown Crust 34
Hawaiian Pancakes 24
Herb-Crusted Lamb Chops with Raspberry Sauce 174
Hot Buffalo, Bacon, Blue Burgers with Celery Salsa 100
Hot Dog Skillet Casserole 152

I
Incredible Bacon-Wrapped Mac and Cheese 88
Individual Pineapple Upside-Down Cakes 240
Individual Pizza Pot Pies 216
Irish Shepherd's Pie with Beef Tenderloin Tips 122
Italian Sausage and Spinach Gnocchi 212

J
Jambalaya with Shrimp and Sausage 190

L
LAMB
Lamb Chops with Garlic-Mint Sauce 172
Herb-Crusted Lamb Chops with Raspberry Sauce 174
LASAGNA
Bacon Cheeseburger Lasagna 218
Lemon Chicken 146
Lime Chicken with Blueberry Bourbon Sauce 124
LOBSTER
Lobster Stuffed with Crab Imperial 196
Seafood Paella 200
Rich and Creamy Lobster Pot Pie 206
Lump Crab Cakes with Chipotle Sauce 182

M
MAC AND CHEESE
Incredible Bacon-Wrapped Mac and Cheese 88
Philly Steak Mac and Cheese 118
Mango Bread 252
Mashed Purple Sweet Potatoes with Coconut Milk, Lime and Ginger 80
Mofongo (Puerto Rican-Style Plantains) 76
Date Nut Pudding 236
Mshikaki Steak Kebabs with Tomato Onion Sauce 116

O
Orange-Ginger Glazed Pork Chops 156
Orange Marmalade Pork Chops 154

P
Palomilla Steak 108
Pan-Seared Salmon with Creamy Cilantro Lime Sauce 198
Pan-Seared Scallops with Lemon Caper Sauce 202
PANCAKES
Hawaiian Pancakes 24
Dutch Baby Pancake with Blackberries and Sliced Almonds 32
Papaya Chicken Curry with Coconut Rice 126

Pastry-Wrapped Baked Brie with Sautéed Plums and Shallots 10
Peanut Butter Cheesecake with Chocolate Graham Cracker Crust 232
Philly Steak Mac and Cheese 118
PIE
Very Berry Pie 242
Pineapple Upside-Down Cakes (Individual) 240
PIZZA
Individual Pizza Pot Pies 216
PORK
Slow Cooker Mojo Pork Roast 148
Caribbean Pork Chops with Spicy Lime-Rum Jerk Sauce 150
Ham and Cheese Casserole with Hash Brown Crust 34
Hot Dog Skillet Casserole 152
Orange Marmalade Pork Chops 154
Orange-Ginger Glazed Pork Chops 156
Root Beer-Glazed Baby Back Ribs 158
Rosemary-Dijon Pork Chops 160
San Francisco Pork Chops 162
Pork Tenderloin with Seared Pears and Shallots 164
Caribbean-Spiced Pork Tenderloin with Pineapple-Mint Salsa 166
Roasted Pork Loin with Apples, Pears and Prunes 168
Black-Eyed Peas with Sausage, Ham Hocks and Bacon 170
Portobello Stuffed Cabbage 84
POTATOES
Baked Mashed Potatoes 74
Festive Fondant Potatoes 78
Mashed Purple Sweet Potatoes with Coconut Milk, Lime and Ginger 80
Buttery, Crispy, Parmesan-Herbed Potato Stacks 86
Classic German Red Cabbage (Rotkohl) 90

R
Remoulade Sauce 12
Rice Noodles with Shrimp and Coconut-Lime Dressing 188
RICE PUDDING
Arroz con Dulce (Puerto Rican Rice Pudding) 234

Rich and Creamy Beef Stroganoff 120
Rich and Creamy Lobster Pot Pie 206
Roasted Beet Salad with Apples, Feta and Candied Walnuts 68
Roasted Pork Loin with Apples, Pears and Prunes 168
Root Beer-Glazed Baby Back Ribs 158
Rosemary-Dijon Pork Chops 160
Rosemary Salmon with Caramelized Oranges 194

S

SALMON
  Rosemary Salmon with Caramelized Oranges 194
  Pan-Seared Salmon with Creamy Cilantro Lime Sauce 198
San Francisco Pork Chops 162
SAUERBRATEN
  German Sauerbraten 112
SAUSAGE
  Baked Ziti with Sausage and Peppers 210
  Italian Sausage and Spinach Gnocchi 212
  Creamy Cajun Chicken Alfredo with Smoked Sausage 214
  Creamy and Cheesey Sausage Potato Soup 52
Savory Ginger Chicken Thighs and Drumsticks 140

SCALLOPS
  Pan-Seared Scallops with Lemon Caper Sauce 202
SCONE
  Cinnamon Apple Scones 248
  Blueberry-Lemon Scones 250
Seafood Paella 200
Sesame-Crusted Tuna with Mango Salsa 178
Sesame-Ginger Chicken 132
SHRIMP RECIPES
  Shrimp Ceviche 16
  Coconut Shrimp with Orange Sauce 180
  Southern Shrimp and Cheesy Grits 184
  Coconut Curry Soup with Shrimp and Mussels 186
  Rice Noodles with Shrimp and Coconut-Lime Dressing 188
  Jambalaya with Shrimp and Sausage 190
  Seafood Paella 200
Slow Cooker Mojo Pork Roast 148
Smoked Salmon Eggs Benedict with Pan-Seared Tomatoes and Asparagus 30
Smoked Sirloin, Brie, Bacon Burgers with Merlot-Portabellos 94
Southern Shrimp and Cheesy Grits 184
SPÄTZLE/SPAETZLE
  German Spätzle/Spaetzle (Tiny Egg Noodle Dumplings) 82

Spicy African Chicken Peanut Stew 40
Spicy Black-Eyed Pea Hummus 20
Spring Greens Salad with Pecan-Crusted Tofu and Mojito Dressing 64
Stir-Fried Beef and Vegetables 110
Sweet and Sour Three-Bean Salad 60

T

Tart (Chocolate Raspberry) 226
Tequila-Lime Chicken Tacos with Creamy Cilantro-Jalapeño Sauce 136
Thanksgiving Turkey Burgers with Stuffing and Cranberry Sauce 102
Tomato Carpaccio with Honey Dijon Vinaigrette 62
TUNA
  Sesame-Crusted Tuna with Mango Salsa 178
  Grilled Ahi Tuna Steak with Bing Cherry Salsa 192

U

U.S. Senate Bean Soup 42

V

Very Berry Pie 242

W

Wasabi Honey Coleslaw 66